'Down to earth, practical and wi[se ...] stillness idea each which gives r[eaders space to explore] and find the one that works best [for their own] hearts and times.'

Rachael Newham, author and theology of mental health specialist

'Lucy's accessible and thoughtful devotional will help you to embrace God's gift of peace and rest – even if your life continues at what feels like a breakneck pace. Birthed out of a year of exploring stillness in the Bible, her guide is filled with engaging scripture and practical suggestions for how to get still and know God. One to make time for.'

Amy Boucher Pye, author of *Holding onto Hope* and spiritual director

'Despite my best intentions, being still in body, mind and soul often eludes me. Relentless demands and problems can distract me from being present to God's presence and promises. Perhaps you can relate, for similar or other reasons. But Lucy has gone ahead of us. She has put into practice and now shares with us her wisdom gleaned from prayerful response to scripture. Her poignant stories, relatable insights, doable suggestions and thought-provoking reflections cover a helpful range of relevant scenarios where "being still" might evade us. Lucy's clear rich writing, her honest vulnerable sharing and at times, her gentle humour, are a gift to help anyone longing to be still yet who feels anything but.'

Anne Le Tissier, speaker, preacher, devotional writer and author of *Dwell*

'We all long to be still and savour God's presence in the chaos of our busy lives, but often can't even begin to see how it's possible. Lucy is an empathetic fellow traveller through life's chaos and the words of her devotional are a wise and welcome guide, helping chronically busy Christians find places in their daily lives to pause and reconnect with God's peace, joy and hope. This is a great, encouraging read, reminding me that stillness can be a daily practice, even in seasons when it feels impossible. I'm grateful for Lucy's wise words and practical, down-to-earth suggestions. I will continue to use them long after I finish the book.'

Georgie Tennant, author of *The God Who Sees*

'I love that *Be Still* has been written by someone as busy as Lucy! It means that the text is totally relatable and honest, as she shares what she has learned after a year of delving into what the Bible has to say about being still. Understanding that most of us have responsibilities we can't lay down, Lucy unpacks why she now believes being still is a state of mind and something we can achieve whatever our circumstances. Lucy is a great writer, and there is much within these pages to encourage as well as challenge. If you want a devotional that will not only fit into your morning routine with ease but provide you with truths to dwell on throughout the day, I heartily recommend *Be Still*.'
Claire Musters, author, speaker, editor and host of the *Woman Alive* book club

'This book is such an encouragement. The tone is perfectly supportive with practical tips and encouragements that never feel overreached. Too often we put pressure on ourselves to strive for perfection in our faith. *Be Still* encourages us to pause and helps us to recognise the value we already bring to the here and now.'
Jack Imbert-Terry, publishing support & development manager, Bible Society

'I read Lucy's book wearing two hats. As a vicar I loved how *Be Still* brought deep truth in Lucy's typical relatable and encouraging way; it read like a friend gently pointing me back to God. But as a parent, I loved that it was realistic! I could actually read it in the brief moments of peace I had to myself. A moment of peace in the beautifully messy reality of family life.'
Andy Baker, priest in charge, St Michael le Belfrey, York

'Compassionate, realistic and Bible-centred – Lucy manages to encourage a habit of stillness without making "Be still" into just another goal to achieve! You have her permission to read this book slowly, giving yourself space to embed just a few of the "stillness ideas" to bring real refreshment into your busy life.'
Lisa Cherrett, editorial project manager, Bible Society

BE STILL

30 DEVOTIONS FOR THOSE WHO FEEL ANYTHING BUT

LUCY RYCROFT

 Ministries

15 The Chambers, Vineyard
Abingdon OX14 3FE
+44 (0)1865 319700 | brf.org.uk

Bible Reading Fellowship (BRF) is a charity (233280) and company limited by guarantee (301324), registered in England and Wales

EU Authorised Representative: Easy Access System Europe – Mustamäe tee 50, 10621 Tallinn, Estonia, **gpsr.requests@easproject.com**

ISBN 978 1 80039 397 4
First published 2025
10 9 8 7 6 5 4 3 2 1 0
All rights reserved

Text © Lucy Rycroft 2025
This edition © Bible Reading Fellowship 2025
Cover illustration and lettering by Rose Edwards, Nodes illustration © Jackie Niam/stock.adobe.com

The author asserts the moral right to be identified as the author of this work

Scripture quotations are taken from The Holy Bible, New International Version (Anglicised edition) copyright © 1979, 1984, 2011 by Biblica. Used by permission of Hodder & Stoughton Publishers, an Hachette UK company. All rights reserved. 'NIV' is a registered trademark of Biblica. UK trademark number 1448790.

Every effort has been made to trace and contact copyright owners for material used in this resource. We apologise for any inadvertent omissions or errors, and would ask those concerned to contact us so that full acknowledgement can be made in the future.

A catalogue record for this book is available from the British Library

Printed and bound by CPI Group (UK) Ltd, Croydon CR0 4YY

LUCY RYCROFT

be still

30 DEVOTIONS FOR THOSE WHO FEEL ANYTHING BUT

BRF Ministries

For my mum, Caroline Baynes, who has always given me the best example of being still in every circumstance.

Photocopying for churches

Please report to CLA Church Licence any photocopy you make from this publication. Your church administrator or secretary will know who manages your CLA Church Licence.

The information you need to provide to your CLA Church Licence administrator is as follows:

Title, Author, Publisher and ISBN

If your church doesn't hold a CLA Church Licence, information about obtaining one can be found at **uk.ccli.com**

CONTENTS

Introduction 9

Day 1	Be still – even when jobs remain undone	12
Day 2	Be still – you can give God everything	16
Day 3	Be still – you are provided for	20
Day 4	Be still – even when life gets busy	24
Day 5	Be still – God can change your mindset	28
Day 6	Be still – in all circumstances	33
Day 7	Be still – focus on your daily provision	37
Day 8	Be still – you know how the story ends	42
Day 9	Be still – even in the midst of chaos	46
Day 10	Be still – right where you are	51
Day 11	Be still – even when you're anxious about money	55
Day 12	Be still – God's given you community	60
Day 13	Be still – you don't need to do it all	64

Day 14	Be still – you don't need to do it all at once	68
Day 15	Be still – the Lord is enough	73
Day 16	Be still – let God provide	77
Day 17	Be still – receive God's good gifts	81
Day 18	Be still – it is God's gift to you	85
Day 19	Be still – observe the sabbath	89
Day 20	Be still – do not conform	93
Day 21	Be still – know your limits	97
Day 22	Be still – receive the joy of the Lord	101
Day 23	Be still – you don't need to be afraid	106
Day 24	Be still – in a world that is not	110
Day 25	Be still – relinquish control	115
Day 26	Be still – the Lord is active	119
Day 27	Be still – take small steps	124
Day 28	Be still – adopt God's priorities	128
Day 29	Be still – even when the future is unknown	132
Day 30	Be still – even when your dreams remain unfulfilled	136

INTRODUCTION

Stillness is an alien concept in today's busy world.

Whatever the time of day or night, there is always somewhere to go, someone to connect with, something to watch or read or listen to. It feels like stillness is a naughty word, with forces combining to ensure that we *never have to be still*. Even with my Scrooge-like approach to TV streaming services, I still have access to thousands of different viewing options at any one time. Take advantage of all of them, and that figure probably heads into five or six figures. My phone alone offers me a seemingly infinite number of podcasts to listen to, articles to read, websites to crawl and people to keep in touch with.

It's not just the digital space that means stillness is hard to come by. There are more and more options of how we spend our free time, where we eat our meals and where we shop – many of which are open much longer hours than they might have been in a previous generation. My children have a huge choice of extracurricular classes, entertainment parks, holiday clubs and leisure activities to choose from. Even the Christian world is not exempt. I've just been to a Christian conference where the number of organisations represented in the exhibition area was staggering, each with a number of different programmes, initiatives and campaigns vying for our time, energy and (let's be honest) money.

Our brains were not designed to cope with such an incessant pace of life. We know that there are well-being benefits to slowing down, enjoying screen-free activities and a good night's sleep. The question is: how do we access these when life's frenetic pace doesn't seem easy to shift?

As a working mum of four children (plus a dog, who's worth another three) and wife of a church leader, I wasn't finding it easy to follow the biblical imperative to 'be still'. To truly live a life of stillness, I'd need to knock off a few members of my family, which (*checks Exodus 20*) would go against another important biblical imperative.

I wanted to find moments to 'be still' within a busy life, so I claimed these words for a year, and went on a journey to discover what the Bible had to say about stillness. Unbeknownst to me at the time, that year was to become the busiest of my life. God was teaching me that stillness was a state of mind as much as a physical state. However, it wasn't long into my journey when I realised that carving out even small pockets of physical stillness would make a difference to my well-being and my relationship with God.

You may have picked up this book because, like me, you are wondering how to slow life down. You may be a chronic overachiever, a Type A personality or a 'busy-holic'. (Welcome to the club!) Or you may be none of those things, but you have a desire to delve deeper into the concept of stillness. I welcome you all. This is my journey of reluctantly laying down a compulsion to do everything, be everywhere and see everyone – and instead to allow God to renew my approach to how I use my time: activity *and* stillness.

I hope that, as we dive into scripture, this will become your journey too.

How to use this book

Each devotion begins with a 'bite-size stillness'. Treat this like a mantra to take into your day – a soundbite of the day's Bible reading.

The 'stillness ideas' at the end of each devotion are optional. Many of them involve embedding a habit over a longer period, and as such I would recommend that you only pick two or three from the whole book which stand out to you.

If you do this devotional on consecutive days throughout a month, it will be impossible to properly embed all the stillness ideas. However, if you spread out the devotionals, doing one per week or per month, you may find yourself being able to attempt more.

DAY 1

Be Still

— even when jobs remain undone.

Introduction

While I've always been a night owl, I can pinpoint – almost to the day – the time in my life when I made a choice to prioritise activity above sleep. I decided that the things I wanted to get done in the day, and what I wanted to do with my life, were worth staying up into the early hours for. A decade later, while I'm definitely improving at going to bed at a reasonable time, I still battle the desire to stay up late to finish a project or just get that last job done. Are you someone who, like me, doesn't like to go to bed without a sense of 'completion'? Or maybe you're an early bird, rising before everyone else in order to crack on with all the things that overwhelm you during the day. If so, today's verse is for you.

Read Psalm 127:2

> In vain you rise early
>   and stay up late,
> toiling for food to eat –
>   for he grants sleep to those he loves.

At the very start of my 'be still' year, this psalm was read out during a sermon at my church. Verse 1 had always been significant in my life, but this time it was verse 2 which stood out, an obvious moment of hearing from God.

We all get 24 hours in the day, but busy people tend to want to cram these to the max. This might be because of a need to prove ourselves, a desire to live life to the full, a struggle to say 'no' or a combination of these factors (and others). We're not so good at setting boundaries for ourselves or realising how much time, headspace and energy a particular commitment might require. So although we know that roughly one-third of our time is supposed to be sleeping, we will often find ourselves stretching our day out as much as we think we can cope with, surviving on less sleep than is healthy.

God says that our attempts to do this are 'in vain'. But if I stay up till midnight folding all the laundry or emptying the dishwasher, then I can come down in the morning to a clean kitchen. That's not in vain. Or if I wake early to catch up with emails, then I can start my working day with a clear inbox. That's not in vain – is it?

The problem is that these jobs don't go away forever. We might have made life a little easier for ourselves in the short term, but in the long term we have created for ourselves a habit that will be hard to break. This is why God says that sacrificing sleep in order to pursue activity is in vain: because the activity will never truly be complete – the dishwasher, laundry basket and inbox will fill up again with new demands on our time – but that night of sleep we sacrificed is not coming back. Promises of going to bed earlier the next night or sleeping in the next morning never actually come to fruition, because we've adopted a mindset of toil, where there will always be a job to do.

In this psalm, the example given is 'toiling for food to eat' – but the application is really *any* activity that ensures our survival (or perceived survival), whether that's literally making meals for our households, keeping on top of the dusting, preparing that Bible study for the house group we lead, or perfecting the project proposal that's due soon. Completing the laundry may ensure you don't have that particular job to do the following day, but you can be sure that we busy people will find another job to fill its role as sleep-displacer.

It is not wrong to work. Paid or unpaid work, in or out of the home, is a God-given gift. But when we absorb a mindset that we cannot rest, cannot be still, until that work is complete, then we have fallen into the trap of working 'in vain'. It is not the work that is the problem, but our attitude towards it. What a kind and compassionate God we have, to give us the gift of sleep.

Prayer

- Are you a night owl or an early bird (or both)? What are the tasks that routinely get in the way when you should be sleeping?

- Ask God to help shift your mindset, teaching you to be still even when there are still things to be done.

Stillness idea

Choose one day or night this week when you're going to be strict about your bedtime. Work back half an hour from when you'd like to be in bed with lights out, and use that as your deadline to do what you need to do. When it gets to that time, stop what you're doing. Leave it undone. Go to bed. If the issue is with early mornings, do this in reverse! Work out when you should ideally be waking up, and set your alarm for then – no earlier.

Reflect

How did that feel? When did you manage to finish that job? Did it set you back? Was it more or less stressful than if you'd sacrificed sleep to complete it?

Be Still

— you can give God everything.

Introduction

Does your busyness make you anxious?

I'm not a natural worrier, but I can tell when I'm overstretched, as I start to feel on edge. Will I be able to successfully juggle all these different commitments? Will I forget an appointment or meeting? Will I be able to be present for my kids when they need me?

In my experience, it's often a vicious circle. You get busy, you start to feel anxious, then the anxiety itself becomes an extra burden and makes you feel even busier. Sometimes, of course, this is a warning sign to us: we need to slow down, reflect on what we're doing and lay a few of our commitments aside. But there may still be many things we *can't* lay aside. The people we care for, the homes we look after, the work which pays the bills. When our responsibilities are causing us anxiety, what biblical truths might help break that cycle?

Read Philippians 4:4–9

> Rejoice in the Lord always. I will say it again: rejoice! Let your gentleness be evident to all. The Lord is near. Do not be anxious about anything, but in every situation, by prayer and petition, with thanksgiving, present your requests to God. And the peace of God, which transcends all understanding, will guard your hearts and your minds in Christ Jesus.
>
> Finally, brothers and sisters, whatever is true, whatever is noble, whatever is right, whatever is pure, whatever is lovely, whatever is admirable – if anything is excellent or praiseworthy – think about such things. Whatever you have learned or received or heard from me, or seen in me – put it into practice. And the God of peace will be with you.

I would love this not to be the case, but when I'm busy any spiritual habits I may have had up to that point are likely to fly out the window. Every spare bit of time is spent trying to keep anxiety at bay by playing 'whack-a-mole' with my never-ending to-do list. So I think it's insightful that this section of Paul's letter to the Philippians, which is about peace, begins with a spiritual habit: 'rejoice' (v. 4). If we are to be people who can truly 'be still' even in seasons of busyness, the first thing we are to do is fix our eyes on the Lord and rejoice in the unchanging goodness of who he is. Our schedules wax and wane, but God is always good in every season.

The second truth is that we are to show our gentleness (v. 5). Note it is assumed we have gentleness. Why? Because it is a fruit of the Spirit, and with the Spirit living in us we have access to the full range of fruit. I think Paul mentions it here because when we are busy, it's easy to be short with people. We are so pushed for time that we become singularly focused on what we need to achieve. Those around us merely become pawns in the game we're trying to complete, rather than dearly beloved human beings designed and valued by God. I can't count the number of times I've been guilty of failing to acknowledge others' needs because

I was so overwhelmed by what I needed to do and how those around me might play their part in my agenda.

After rejoicing in the Lord and showing gentleness to others, we get a reminder: 'The Lord is near' (v. 5). I usually take a breath at this point when reading this passage to let the beauty of those words sink in. What a privilege, that the creator of the universe, the God of all things, the redeemer of humankind should draw near to us! Within this context, we can now be reminded to 'not be anxious about anything, but… present your requests to God' (v. 6).

I love that Paul doesn't simply tell us not to worry but gives us something practical to do to help. Often as busy people, we can think that God is not interested in the minutiae of our day or that we should save our prayer time for more significant issues, like our friend who is awaiting test results or a terrible war going on elsewhere in the world. These things need our prayers too – but we don't need to have perfect prayer lives before we ask God to help with every detail of our lives. A regular prayer of mine – particularly when my work list doesn't seem to match the number of waking hours in the day – is that God 'accelerates' my work, or draws out the hours, so that I can complete what I need to in the time I have. You can pray for your child to nap, your spouse to get home early from work, dinner to be made in half the time (or, better still, that a kind friend might drop some food round!), a miraculous slot of time to be opened up so that you can tidy up before your guests arrive, a full night's sleep on less-than-a-full-night's hours… God can do the miraculous! We can literally give every aspect of our busyness to him.

And the result? Peace (vv. 7, 9). God's incomprehensible peace which leaves you feeling still even when you're storming through life at 90 miles per hour. How can that be? It doesn't make logical sense! It 'transcends all understanding' (v. 7) because it's not dependent on our outward circumstances, but in what God is doing in our hearts. Turning our eyes to him in praise (v. 4), allowing his gentleness to work its way out (v. 5), remembering his presence (v. 5) and fixing our minds on what is true (v. 8) all help us truly give our busyness over to him. If we can discipline ourselves to do these things every day, we will know what it means to be still, regardless of what our calendar looks like.

Prayer

- Consider the commands from today's passage: rejoice; be gentle; remember the Lord is near; present your requests to God; fix your mind on what is true. Which of these do you find most of a challenge right now?

- Ask God to come and change your heart in this area. Ask him to help you with what you're struggling with. Ask him to bring his peace 'which transcends all understanding' right now.

Stillness idea

Take the command you picked out in the prayer prompt. Write it out and place it on your bedside table or somewhere you'll see first thing each morning. Start each day by following this command. 'Rejoice' might look like reading out a psalm or using your own words to praise God for who he is. 'Be gentle' might look like asking God to fill you with this particular fruit. 'Remember the Lord is near' might involve a minute of silence or deep breathing as you acknowledge God's presence within you.

Reflect

Has this morning habit made an impact on the rest of your day? If so, how? Is it something you feel you could/should keep doing? Or will you pick a different command to try?

Be Still

— you are provided for.

Introduction

My personal journey of learning to 'be still' has been in the context of a season of life which, despite my best efforts, will always be busy.

Rather than resent the people God has put in our lives to love and care for, the home he has given us which requires upkeep, or the sometimes-stressful jobs he has provided in order for us to pay the bills and use our gifts, we want to be disciples who find God's stillness *within* busyness.

Stillness is a mindset as much as it is a practice. Sometimes busyness can't be avoided – but God can still bring stillness in the midst of it. Today's psalm reminds us of this.

Read Psalm 23

The Lord is my shepherd, I lack nothing.
   He makes me lie down in green pastures,
he leads me beside quiet waters,
   he refreshes my soul.
He guides me along the right paths
   for his name's sake.
Even though I walk
   through the darkest valley,
I will fear no evil,
   for you are with me;
your rod and your staff,
   they comfort me.

You prepare a table before me
   in the presence of my enemies.
You anoint my head with oil;
   my cup overflows.
Surely your goodness and love will follow me
   all the days of my life,
and I will dwell in the house of the Lord
   forever.

You might be able to churn out these familiar words by heart, but have you taken them to heart? I know I often struggle to live the truths this beautiful psalm contains.

Sometimes our busyness has arisen out of a fear of not having enough. We work hard to get a promotion or build our side hustle or research where to invest our money, just in case God doesn't provide what we need. But this psalm reminds us that God is looking after us, which means we have everything we need (v. 1). The sheep don't worry where they're going next, what they're going to eat or what happens when a wolf comes; they completely trust the care of their shepherd.

Sometimes our busyness makes us stressed, tired or even ill. But this is not God's plan for us. He knows we need rest – physically and emotionally (vv. 2–3). Will we accept it when he provides it for us?

Sometimes our busyness is self-induced: we haven't listened to where God's leading us, so we take on all manner of new commitments and activities which end up wearing us down. But verse 3 reassures us that, when we listen to him, God will guide us down the right paths. He will give us a sense of when to say 'yes' and when to say 'no' to different offers. Many of the women in our church right now are preparing to go away together for a weekend, and if I'm honest, I'm sad not to be joining them. Months ago, I was asked to lead worship at this weekend. I love leading worship, and who doesn't love a weekend away from their kids? (I also love my kids, for clarity.) But God gave me foresight of how busy this year was shaping up to be, foresight I don't think I'd have had on my own. I said 'no' – regretfully – but know now that it was the right decision.

Sometimes our busyness feels dark and overwhelming (vv. 4–5). We want a way out, but there's no easy option. Some things need wading through. But this psalm reminds us of God's presence, comfort and anointing during hard times. We can know stillness in the dark times too.

It *is* possible to be still, even within a hectic, full, non-stop life. It might not look a whole lot like physical stillness – although it's important to have that sometimes – but knowing God is our provider, our rest-giver, our navigator and our comfort gives us a peace as we go about our crammed, active days. Our attitude of stillness within busyness will point others to the God who longs to provide for them too.

Prayer

- Pick a phrase from this psalm that particularly speaks to you in the season you're in.

- Read it several times, offer it to the Lord and ask him to help you absorb and live this truth.

Stillness idea

There are many musical settings of this psalm, from Crimond to Stuart Townend to Howard Goodall, all freely available on YouTube or Spotify. Play one that you like, and spend a few minutes listening to the words, meditating particularly on the phrase you chose in the prayer exercise and praying it into your day's activities.

Reflect

How is God working this truth into your life? How is it affecting your attitude towards what you have to do each day?

Be Still

— even when life gets busy.

Introduction

How do you cope in times of increased busyness? I tend to write copious lists, multitask as much as possible, combine errands where I can and liaise with my husband to make sure we're both operating at maximum efficiency. If I'm honest, I'm not sure how much I let God in to exercise his strength through my weakness.

In this passage, the Israelites have just been released from their life of slavery in Egypt. However, a season that should have been marked by freedom and joy becomes a time of stress for them when Pharaoh changes his mind about letting them go and chases after them with an army of thousands.

Read Exodus 14:10–22

As Pharaoh approached, the Israelites looked up, and there were the Egyptians, marching after them. They were terrified and cried out to the Lord. They said to Moses, 'Was it because there were no graves in Egypt that you brought us to the desert to die? What have you done to us by bringing us out of Egypt? Didn't we say to you in Egypt, "Leave us alone; let us serve the Egyptians"? It would have been better for us to serve the Egyptians than to die in the desert!'

Moses answered the people, 'Do not be afraid. Stand firm and you will see the deliverance the Lord will bring you today. The Egyptians you see today you will never see again. The Lord will fight for you; you need only to be still.'

Then the Lord said to Moses, 'Why are you crying out to me? Tell the Israelites to move on. Raise your staff and stretch out your hand over the sea to divide the water so that the Israelites can go through the sea on dry ground. I will harden the hearts of the Egyptians so that they will go in after them. And I will gain glory through Pharaoh and all his army, through his chariots and his horsemen. The Egyptians will know that I am the Lord when I gain glory through Pharaoh, his chariots and his horsemen.'

Then the angel of God, who had been travelling in front of Israel's army, withdrew and went behind them. The pillar of cloud also moved from in front and stood behind them, coming between the armies of Egypt and Israel. Throughout the night the cloud brought darkness to the one side and light to the other side; so neither went near the other all night long.

Then Moses stretched out his hand over the sea, and all that night the Lord drove the sea back with a strong east wind and turned it into dry land. The waters were divided, and the Israelites went through the sea on dry ground, with a wall of water on their right and on their left.

If it wasn't hard enough to lead thousands of people and animals from one country to another on foot, Moses now finds his people being hotly pursued by the Egyptian army. His job is to pivot to a motivational speaker and lift the spirits of the complaining Israelites.

The advice Moses gives in verses 13 and 14 is both encouraging ('Do not be afraid'; 'Stand firm') and prophetic ('The deliverance the Lord will bring you'; 'The Egyptians you see today you will never see again'). These are not glib platitudes, but confident declarations of what the Lord is going to do. Moses' relationship with God is such that he can be totally confident of victory in this seemingly desperate situation.

However, there is one piece of advice Moses gives which is just plain confusing: 'The Lord will fight for you; you need only to be still.' Excuse me? It takes a lot of faith to be able to proclaim victory before it has happened – but victory which apparently doesn't take any effort from the Israelites? Has Moses gone mad?

Let's look a little more closely at this command to the Israelites to 'be still' – after all, the Israelites are not *physically* still: they are commanded to move on, to walk through the sea on the dry land God opens up for them. Stillness here does not mean inaction.

The Hebrew word translated here as 'still' is *charash*, which relates to being silent and holding your peace. The Israelites must play their part in their victory – walking forward – but they are not to call out curses on the Egyptians, to declare war or to fight. The Lord will enable them to travel safely and remain protected from the Egyptians, while ensuring that the Egyptians are not able to pursue them again. He doesn't ask his people to do anything other than what they are able to do in this situation: to move forward in faith. He will do the rest.

What is your default when heading into a week that's chock-full of appointments, meetings and engagements? What is your natural response when dealing with a stressful situation? If, like me, you feel you're shouldering the burden of absolutely everything associated with that particular event or challenge, this passage comes as a welcome relief. God only requires of us that we move forward in faith. He does not need us to fight, nor does he need us to take on ourselves the responsibility for success. We can leave it in God's hands – which, in turn, means we can stop and be still, even in the busiest of weeks.

Prayer

- Consider your current week/month. Where are the pain points, the struggles and the things that make life busy?

- Take these to God. For each one, ask him what he would have you do. Allow space for him to communicate with you.

- Finally, ask that his strength would work supernaturally through what you're able to contribute to the situation, and that he would give you moments of stillness and rest throughout this time.

Stillness idea

Choose one thing that's making life busy or stressful right now. Each time you think about that thing, train yourself to turn to God first. See if you can be still with him for one minute before thinking or worrying about the situation. This may take some practice! Define 'stillness' as whatever is appropriate in the situation. If you're lying in bed at night, you can be physically and mentally still. If you're driving, don't close your eyes! But perhaps switching off the radio and leaning in to what God might be saying would be an appropriate act of stillness.

Reflect

How is God changing your heart towards the stressor that you're bringing to him? Has your perspective shifted?

DAY 5

Be Still

— God can change your mindset.

Introduction

As a busy person, I'm often under the naive impression that things will be easier/quieter/more relaxed in the future. Do you ever find yourself thinking this too?

When I was a busy teacher in my 20s, I thought this utopian moment of freedom would arrive with the advent of children, especially if I was able to take some years out of work to focus on them. But my life soon filled up with baby classes, new friends, setting up groups and hosting them – as well as, you know, the small job of caring for a new baby. 'It's fine,' I told myself. 'One day these babies will grow up and go to school, and then my life will be much less frenetic.' Cue the PTA, school events, after-school activities, playdates and parties. These days I often think how peaceful life will be in retirement – but I'm aware that there will, again, be many things to fill my days: serving at church and in the community, caring for potential grandchildren, increased medical appointments and possibly a continuation of some paid work too.

Life will always be busy, because at every stage our culture is throwing ideas at us for how to spend our time. There simply aren't enough lives to do everything we could possibly do. I am learning that busyness is a mindset, not a state of being. The good news is that God can change our mindset so that even in busy seasons we will know the peace and joy of stillness.

Read Mark 4:35–41

> That day when evening came, he said to his disciples, 'Let us go over to the other side.' Leaving the crowd behind, they took him along, just as he was, in the boat. There were also other boats with him. A furious squall came up, and the waves broke over the boat, so that it was nearly swamped. Jesus was in the stern, sleeping on a cushion. The disciples woke him and said to him, 'Teacher, don't you care if we drown?'
>
> He got up, rebuked the wind and said to the waves, 'Quiet! Be still!' Then the wind died down and it was completely calm.
>
> He said to his disciples, 'Why are you so afraid? Do you still have no faith?'
>
> They were terrified and asked each other, 'Who is this? Even the wind and the waves obey him!'

Jesus is exhausted. He suggests to the disciples that they go out in the boat to the other side of the lake, to have some time away from the crowd he has been faithfully teaching, and promptly falls asleep in the boat.

I find it fascinating that although Jesus is leading the disciples to peace and rest on the opposite side of the lake, as far as the disciples are concerned, he has led them into *danger*. What's going on?

There is a destination here that Jesus wants to reach, both for him and for his disciples. The destination is away from the incessant crowds who won't leave him alone. Jesus' role is to teach them, but he needs rest to be able to fulfil this role, which is why he suggests the boat trip. What happens on the way is not part of the plan. Jesus' idea is for rest and recuperation, but within a fallen world, this doesn't turn out the way the disciples expected.

God does not lead us into danger. But the broken world in which we operate is full of it. We might be carrying out a role God has led us into, but something about it is hard or even dangerous. We've prayed many times, wondering if it's right to give this up, because it doesn't seem to be working out very well, but still God tells us to carry on.

How do we know God can bring stillness to our busy or anxious minds? Because he can do it for the wind and the waves. The Greek word used in verse 39 is *phimŏō*, which means 'to muzzle'. Just as we might place a muzzle over the mouth of a dog, Jesus is able to muzzle the storm. He is able to tame and train it as we might do an animal.

As a child I remember singing a song that went, 'With Jesus in the boat, we can smile at the storm.' Within that cringeworthy tweeness lies a challenging and insightful truth: God does not promise there will not be storms, but he does promise us the presence of Jesus in our boat, muzzling the storms as we travel together. Jesus was able to sleep, even through a life-threatening storm. Lord, give us that ability to trust you when all around us is turbulent!

Perhaps you are travelling through a 'storm' right now: a challenging season of ill health, financial worries, relational difficulties or something else with no clear end in sight. But perhaps the 'storm' is simply that our own busy mindset refuses to shift. We are feeling worn down and on the brink of burn-out with all we have to do, yet we have little hope that we will ever stop being Busy People. It's a label we've worn all our lives which seems impossible to shake off, regardless of age or stage.

Jesus has good news for those of us with busy mindsets. Just as he muzzled the tossings and turnings of the wind and waves when he was in the boat with the disciples, so he can muzzle the turbulent minds of busy people who find it hard to switch off. He can bring sleep where there has been insomnia, peace where there has been anxiety and the ability to say 'no' where there have previously been no boundaries.

Prayer

- Can you think of a time in your life when you weren't busy? If so, what was different then to now? If not, do you feel you have a 'busy mindset' which seems impossible to shift? Is your busyness situational, because you're in a busy season, or can you tell that it's more of a chronic condition than that?

- Bring your mindset to God. Acknowledge that he is in the business of renewing our minds (Romans 12:2). Do you trust that he can renew yours? Ask him to do so now.

Stillness idea

Define the end of your 'working week'. This could be the closing of your laptop on a Friday afternoon, the moment the kids are in bed on Friday evening, or any other time when you feel that one week is about to end and another begin. It is always tempting to get going with the next task – whether that's making dinner, seeing your spouse or getting ready to go out with friends – but the importance of this idea is all in resisting the urge to move quickly on, so be firm with yourself!

At your designated point, set a timer for ten minutes and lie on your bed. You can play soft meditative music if you find it helpful to relax or just lie in silence. Resist the urge to think or pray about anything particular, but just use the time to be physically still, relaxing your mind and body, before continuing with your day.

Reflect

How did this small piece of stillness affect you? How did it change your attitude going into the next part of your day or week? How can you build in more moments of peaceful resting, knowing that Jesus is in the boat with you?

Be Still

– in all circumstances.

Introduction

Our lives are very changeable. We go through busy seasons and less busy seasons, work in different jobs, journey through different seasons of family life, have different relationships, live in different places.

But being still before God should not be a changeable feature of our lives. My journey of learning to be still while leading a seemingly unstill life has opened my heart to the universal nature of God's call. I believe that, with his strength and by his Spirit, we can learn to be still *in all circumstances*, whether busy or bored, parenting multiple children or wondering whether we'll ever get two lines on the pregnancy test, happily single or praying for a partner, stimulated in a busy job or frustrated by an unsympathetic boss. Following on from our passage on day 2, Paul goes on to share some powerful words about how this can be possible.

Read Philippians 4:10-13

> I rejoiced greatly in the Lord that at last you renewed your concern for me. Indeed, you were concerned, but you had no opportunity to show it. I am not saying this because I am in need, for I have learned to be content whatever the circumstances. I know what it is to be in need, and I know what it is to have plenty. I have learned the secret of being content in any and every situation, whether well fed or hungry, whether living in plenty or in want. I can do all this through him who gives me strength.

In my first job as a music teacher, I worked under a wonderful Christian head of department who remains a special friend. He was an incredible musician and a fabulously fun character – the type of teacher you never forget – but would be the first to tell you that being organised was not his gifting. We had a very haphazard store-cupboard-cum-office in between our classrooms, which just felt burdensome every time we or the students entered. My head of department would regularly declare that as soon as we got this-or-that out of the way, we would get the cupboard sorted out, with proper labels for everything, and that this would make life a lot easier because of *x, y* and z. I totally believed him, and I'm sure he believed it too when he said it, but of course our good intentions rarely came to fruition. On the odd occasions they did, the mess soon returned.

I think we can often spend our lives thinking that as soon as we've done this or eliminated that, as soon as our kids have grown or we've bought a house, we will have a bit more time to pursue God. But that time never comes – or, rather, when it does it brings with it unforeseen complications which make our intended goal just as impossible. Living in the future in this way – hoping that a time further down the line will be easier/less busy/more enjoyable – means that we miss out on what God is doing *now*.

These words of Paul's are so wise for our fast-moving times. Paul experienced a lot of hardship: persecution, ridicule, arrests, imprisonment, a 'thorn in his side' (which might have been a physical or mental illness), the uncertainty of living by faith and even a shipwreck. It must have been tempting to think, 'Well, as soon as I'm out of this prison, I'll get back to preaching,' or, 'Once I'm back on dry land I'll think about God again.' Yet he realised that there was no 'perfect' time to draw close to God, no ideal moment in which faith would be something easy to live out. To believe that there was would be to assume a future he didn't yet know. Living his life for God meant being able to find contentment and peace at every turn. His secret? 'Him who gives me strength' (v. 13).

The irony for a lot of us busy Christians is that while we're holding out for a better moment in life to really drill down into our relationship with God, we're simultaneously trying to find contentment in our own strength. As the old hymn goes: 'Oh what peace we often forfeit, oh what needless pain we bear, all because we do not carry everything to God in prayer.' Perhaps it might be wise to look to God as our source of stillness, inviting him to work his strength in our busy lives.

Although our music cupboard-office never really got sorted out, I'm so pleased my head of department didn't put everything on hold until it did. We'd have missed out on giving the students some really amazing musical opportunities: performing in ensembles, going on tour to France, enjoying visiting musicians and learning from an engaging and robust curriculum. The department wasn't perfect, but it was able to grow and flourish because my boss didn't allow a frustrating situation to hold him back.

Similarly, as busy people, let's not allow our messy, over-scheduled, tiring lives to control us. We don't need to wait until we can devote 30 minutes of each morning to Bible reading and intercessory prayer – although if you're already doing this then all power to you. But in any way we can, let us reach out to the God who made us and knows us better than we do. Let's open our eyes to what he is doing through our busyness, our ears to how he may be encouraging and challenging us, and offer up our imperfect-but-soft hearts to be shaped and moulded by him.

Prayer

- Have you ever felt that it might be easier to connect with God in a future season of your life? How do you feel about that? Do you feel that season will come? Will it look like you're imagining it now?

- Take your 'now' to God. Ask him to draw close to you *now*, with all you have to do. Ask him to teach you how to be still before him *now*. Ask him to work in your life *now* and show you ways of connecting with him *now*.

Stillness idea

Many of us have been taught a particular way of connecting with God: a conventional 'quiet time' which happens in the morning, is always quiet, involves the Bible and includes time for prayer. This is not a bad model, but it is restrictive, and can make those of us who struggle with this habit feel like we can't connect with God at all. If this is you, think of a new connection point you could have with God each day: perhaps a scripture verse on your wall which you'll read each time you walk past, saying the Lord's Prayer in the shower, or listening to worship music as you travel to work. Try this out for a few days.

Reflect

Which connection habit did you try? How is it going? How easy or difficult are you finding it to implement regularly? If it's not working, what other habit could you try?

DAY 7

Be Still

— focus on daily provision.

Introduction

When faced with a busy season – whether that's a time-consuming work project, a church event we're organising or a season of navigating hospital visits – it is easy to lose sight of the day-to-day work in favour of the size of the problem facing us. The date looms closer and we wonder: will everything get done? Are we prepared? Will others pull their weight? How successful will this be? How will I come across to others?

I am writing this book in such a season. I'm in the process of transitioning back to my first career of teaching, alternating days in the classroom with days at my current job. I will be attempting to complete a hefty work project for my existing employer in only half the work hours, while also relearning my former career. All five members of my family have their birthdays and accompanying celebrations within this period.

What is the good news of Jesus in my overwhelming period of busyness and in yours?

Read Exodus 16:13–24

That evening quail came and covered the camp, and in the morning there was a layer of dew around the camp. When the dew was gone, thin flakes like frost on the ground appeared on the desert floor. When the Israelites saw it, they said to each other, 'What is it?' For they did not know what it was.

Moses said to them, 'It is the bread the Lord has given you to eat. This is what the Lord has commanded: "Everyone is to gather as much as they need. Take an omer for each person you have in your tent."'

The Israelites did as they were told; some gathered much, some little. And when they measured it by the omer, the one who gathered much did not have too much, and the one who gathered little did not have too little. Everyone had gathered just as much as they needed.

Then Moses said to them, 'No one is to keep any of it until morning.'

However, some of them paid no attention to Moses; they kept part of it until morning, but it was full of maggots and began to smell. So Moses was angry with them.

Each morning everyone gathered as much as they needed, and when the sun grew hot, it melted away. On the sixth day, they gathered twice as much – two omers for each person – and the leaders of the community came and reported this to Moses. He said to them, 'This is what the Lord commanded: "Tomorrow is to be a day of sabbath rest, a holy sabbath to the Lord. So bake what you want to bake and boil what you want to boil. Save whatever is left and keep it until morning."'

So they saved it until morning, as Moses commanded, and it did not stink or get maggots in it.

Perhaps the Israelites weren't 'busy' in the sense we consider ourselves to be in the 21st century. But we can easily believe they were overwhelmed by the task ahead of them: walking through the desert for 40 years or more – in some cases, a whole lifetime, in search of the 'promised land'. When would they reach it? Was it going to be better than their life in Egypt? Was Moses telling the truth? Was God really leading them? Or would this all turn out to be folly? I can understand why they were frustrated and grumpy.

All the Israelites can see is the wide expanse of desert, and the very real possibility that they will all die shortly (16:3), even though God has provided what they needed so far. They don't need a change in situation; they need a change in perspective – and they get it through the daily provision of manna and quail. Every morning, the ground is littered with manna – white, wafer-like food that will sustain them through the day. But the key thing is not *what* is provided, but *how* it is provided: each day, enough to sustain them until the next.

I'm writing this in an Asian café, eating a delicious Japanese bento box. For me, food is one of God's greatest gifts, and I enjoy pretty much all of it. Cooking it and enjoying others' cooking brings me a huge amount of pleasure. I can't imagine, therefore, how the Israelites could have eaten the same thing each day for *forty years* (16:35). I expect that, had Moses delivered this timeframe to them at the start of their manna journey, they'd have been less than impressed. But isn't this the point? We don't know what lies ahead of us – and, largely, this is for our benefit, as we probably wouldn't be too impressed if we knew what was coming either! God doesn't ask us to accept a detailed plan of the rest of our lives, but to trust him to provide in every season.

God makes it very clear that each person is only to collect what they need *for that day*. As soon as they start to hoard it for the next day, it goes bad. Why? Because God is calling them to trust that he will be faithful tomorrow, as he has been today. Only on the day before the sabbath does he provide a double amount which doesn't turn stale – a reminder that even in the overwhelming task the Israelites have ahead of them, they are still to take a day of rest.

There is a deep kind of peace which comes when we realise God is providing each day what we need in order to scale the challenge in front of us. Rather than be overwhelmed by the looming deadline or anxiety over how things will be when the expected life-change happens, we can look at the day ahead, at the time God has given us for planning and preparation, at the people he has given us to help and support us, at the hours he has given us for rest and sleep, and know that, whatever the challenge, he's absolutely got this.

Prayer

- Think of a particular project, activity, relationship or other responsibility which seems overwhelming to you right now. Consider the timeframe – is there a deadline? An obvious end in sight? Or do you have no idea right now when this will draw to a close?

- Ask God to take the overwhelm and instead show you where you can make small, incremental steps towards it *today*. Ask him to continue to give you what you need daily, as well as opportunity for rest (and the good sense to take it!).

Stillness idea

Take what you thought of in the prayer activity above and write it out on a piece of paper or sticky note. Place it somewhere visible near your bed. (If it is a more personal or sensitive item, you may want to hide it from prying eyes!)

Each morning, as you spot this challenge, commit it to God, asking that he will give you what you need towards it *today*. Try to get into the habit of committing this to God at the start of each day until it has finished.

Reflect

How are you feeling now about this project or season? Have you found that committing it to God each morning helps remove some of the overwhelm? How is the project progressing? How have you seen God providing daily what you need to complete it?

Be Still

— you know how the story ends.

Introduction

One of the ways we can be still even in busy, stressful weeks or seasons is by remembering that this life isn't all there is. By fixing our eyes on the hope we have of Jesus' return to earth, and the subsequent restoration of everything to how God originally intended it to be, we gain a perspective that puts our earthly tasks in their rightful place.

Read Revelation 21:1–8

> Then I saw 'a new heaven and a new earth,' for the first heaven and the first earth had passed away, and there was no longer any sea. I saw the Holy City, the new Jerusalem, coming down out of heaven from God, prepared as a bride beautifully dressed for her husband. And I heard a loud voice from the throne saying, 'Look! God's dwelling-place is now among the people, and he will dwell with them. They will be his people, and God himself will be with them and be their God. "He will wipe every

> tear from their eyes. There will be no more death" or mourning or crying or pain, for the old order of things has passed away.'
>
> He who was seated on the throne said, 'I am making everything new!' Then he said, 'Write this down, for these words are trustworthy and true.'
>
> He said to me: 'It is done. I am the Alpha and the Omega, the Beginning and the End. To the thirsty I will give water without cost from the spring of the water of life. Those who are victorious will inherit all this, and I will be their God and they will be my children. But the cowardly, the unbelieving, the vile, the murderers, the sexually immoral, those who practise magic arts, the idolaters and all liars – they will be consigned to the fiery lake of burning sulphur. This is the second death.'

In November 2003, my church held an all-day event on a Saturday. But as the date drew nearer, England made such progress in the Rugby World Cup that they ended up in the final – which was scheduled for the same day as our church event. Held in Australia, the match was happening first thing in the morning for us, so our vicar, a keen rugby fan and chaplain of the local rugby team, asked someone to record the match at home while we were in church. He extended the lunch break so that anyone interested could watch the match then, as if live.

Just before the break, he went to set up the video that had been left in a side room. Assuming it would be set to the start of the game, he pressed play – only to see the final frame of Martin Johnson lifting the Webb Ellis Cup for England. Keeping quiet about the fact he knew the result, he sat and watched the match with everyone else. However, while the conclusion was a certainty, he didn't know how we'd get there: that the match would go into extra time and that the final few seconds would be so crucial, with a now-famous drop goal. He got to experience the excitement of that game along with everyone else.

It is much easier for us to enjoy life when we have the peace of knowing how things will turn out – and, as Christians, we do! This passage in Revelation reminds us that one day Jesus will come again. When he does, God will create 'a new heaven and a new earth' (v. 1), dwell with us (v. 3) and wipe every tear from our eyes (v. 4). What a wonderful image!

When we are weighed down with the care of another person or with work that seems to get more stressful every year, we can remember that one day all of it will be restored. There will be no 'death or mourning or crying or pain' (v. 4), so caring for one another will be a joy and never a burden. Our work will not be 'in vain', working instead towards goals and purposes that are fully realised (Isaiah 65:21–23). If we feel resentful that life has ended up harder than we would have liked, we can rest assured that our reward is coming. Better than a luxury five-star holiday, our life in heaven will be perfect in every way: perfect bodies, perfect relationships, perfect creation. None of the things which cause us stress or hardship in this life will exist in the same way in heaven: sin will be eradicated and all else restored.

This isn't to say that we treat this life flippantly. We are called to work diligently and obediently in the places God has put us. Our earthly lives are when we get to grow in holiness, learn from the Father and become shaped to be more like the Son. We don't want to miss out on what God is doing in us and through us as we carry out our daily tasks. But we also don't need to be consumed by what is around us. We can be still even in the busiest seasons, because we know that this life is not all there is. One day we will live with God forever, and until then we are in rehearsal. Learning to let God into our busyness, shaping us and causing us to be still before him, will grow us to the point where eventually we'll hear the words, 'Well done, good and faithful servant' (Matthew 25:21).

Prayer

- Has any aspect of your life become overwhelming recently? An elderly parent, a child's diagnosis, a situation at work or church?

- Bring this before God now. Ask him to give you his eternal perspective on the situation. Invite his wisdom of what is going on in the spiritual realm as you battle on earth.

Stillness idea

It is hard to gain perspective on life when we are consumed by daily tasks. Try stepping outside today for five minutes – whatever the weather – and being still in nature. Even if you're in an urban area, you still have the sky to enjoy. Allow your perspective to be shifted by the knowledge that God's creation is vast, and he is concerned for it all – including the things which weigh you down.

Reflect

How does this activity bring clarity and lightness to what you are going through today?

DAY 9

Be Still

– even in the midst of chaos.

Introduction

The month in which I submitted the proposal for this book was a busy one. In addition to my normal workload, I had two book proposals to submit, a new course to launch, a presentation to make to trustees and an eight-hour round trip to lead a day for our freelance team. At home, my youngest was booked in for an operation, my eldest was going to Italy with his school, my middle son and daughter had gym competitions in different places on the same day, and my daughter also had a dance performance in another town. Unusually for a clergy spouse, I was away for two weekends. When I then discovered that I had a full-day interview for a teaching job – a career I hadn't touched for over a decade, and for which there would be a significant amount of preparation – I had to laugh, otherwise I might have cried!

The psalm we're reading today has plenty to say to those of us whose lives sometimes feel chaotic and impossible.

Read Psalm 46

God is our refuge and strength,
    an ever-present help in trouble.
Therefore we will not fear, though the earth give way
    and the mountains fall into the heart of the sea,
though its waters roar and foam
    and the mountains quake with their surging.

There is a river whose streams make glad the city of God,
    the holy place where the Most High dwells.
God is within her, she will not fall;
    God will help her at break of day.
Nations are in uproar, kingdoms fall;
    he lifts his voice, the earth melts.

The Lord Almighty is with us;
    the God of Jacob is our fortress.

Come and see what the Lord has done,
    the desolations he has brought on the earth.
He makes wars cease
    to the ends of the earth.
He breaks the bow and shatters the spear;
    he burns the shields with fire.
He says, 'Be still, and know that I am God;
    I will be exalted among the nations,
    I will be exalted in the earth.'

The Lord Almighty is with us;
    the God of Jacob is our fortress.

This psalm is full of chaos – did you notice? The earth gives way, the mountains fall into the sea, the waters are in turmoil, there's some kind of earthquake going on, nations are in uproar and kingdoms are falling. It makes my chaotic family life look like an advert for a spa day.

And yet look at how the psalm begins and ends: with confident declarations of God's presence with us. We don't need to fear even the most chaotic, earth-shattering disasters, because God is our refuge, our strength and our help. The psalm ends with a picture of God as our fortress. He keeps us safe, he gives us fortified protection, and we don't need to fear what might be happening around us.

God is not only *with* us, however. Verse 5 reminds us that he is also *within* us. Initially, those listening to this psalm would have read this as God being in Jerusalem (the 'city of God', v. 4), but the New Testament confirms that, since Jesus' death tore the temple curtain in two, *we* are now God's temple, the place where he lives (1 Corinthians 3:16).

What does this mean? It means that the one strong enough to hold an entire city up is also holding us up – not by pulling our arms so that we can't fall, but because he is *in* us, giving us a far firmer internal foundational structure. It means that the one whose voice makes the earth melt (v. 6) is also speaking to and through us. It means that the one capable of ending wars and breaking weapons (vv. 9–10) is at work in our own personal battles.

We serve a God who is powerful for good in this chaotic world and in our chaotic lives. The command in verse 10, then, to 'be still' is entirely feasible. The Hebrew word used for 'still' in this psalm is *râphâh*, which means to slacken, cease or even be weakened. The psalmist is calling us to lean into our weakness and frailty, to lean back into the strength of the one who can melt the earth simply by raising his voice.

When life gets chaotic, what does the world tell us to do? Write lists. Utilise an organisational app. Delegate. Drop some balls. Lose some sleep. Use this system or that process. In other words: do whatever you can to stay strong, hold it all together, keep succeeding, look the part. Psalm 46 tells us the opposite: do whatever you can to remember your weakness, throwing the chaos on to God and allowing his strength – which is within you – to work mightily.

What I realised in my busy month was that our own abilities only go so far. I felt particularly weak, because there was so much going on that I couldn't give 100% to everything, otherwise I would have burned out. I realise now that this month was an act of God's grace, giving me no choice but to rely on his strength to fill the gap between what I was able to bring and what was needed. The result? Two accepted book proposals; a course launch that smashed our target; success in the presentation, training day and operation; two incredibly special weekends away with family and friends; my kids' enjoyment of their activities – and I got the job. No credit to me, all glory to the God who is our 'ever-present help in trouble'.

Prayer

- Are you feeling life is running out of control right now? Have you had a season like this recently or are you anticipating a week/month coming up which might be a little more chaotic?

- Take it to the Lord, leaning in to your weakness and asking him to fill the gap between what you feel physically and emotionally able to do and what is needed in order for life to happen.

Stillness idea

It takes discipline to bring things to God, rather than do them in our own strength. I'll be honest, I don't find it easy until I'm really brought to my knees, like I was in the month I described. But we can train ourselves to submit our schedules to God, by getting specific about what we want him to do. Next time you're writing a list of tasks or starting a busy day or week, try telling God exactly what you would love to be the outcome of each task. You might say, 'Please help me prepare this presentation in one hour, because I'm not sure what other time I'm going to have,' or, 'Please help my child feel confident in this competition that I can't be at with them.' God doesn't always act in the way we want him to – he is God – but he is always present, always listens and is always working for our ultimate good, even when we can't see it yet.

Reflect

When the tasks are done or the busy day is over, go back over your list. What did God do exactly as you'd asked him? What did he do better? What remains a mystery? You may like to journal these and use them as the basis for praise and thanksgiving.

DAY 10

Be Still
— right where you are.

Introduction

When you're at peak busyness, I wonder if you ever dream of a time or a place where you could be fully refreshed? I'm writing this two weeks away from our family holiday, and I'll happily admit that it's the thought of long, lingering days spent in nature with the people I love most that's providing motivation to do my day job, prepare for my new job and write this book. I'm working hard, knowing that at the end of it, I'll be rewarded with beautiful Scottish lochs, rugged landscapes and unspoilt islands.

Rest is one of God's greatest gifts to us, and I don't think it's any coincidence that his beautiful creation is often where we find ourselves restored and strengthened. But today's reading reminds us that there is a place where we find true, long-lasting refreshment – and we don't need to wait for our annual leave or family holiday to find it.

Read Psalm 84:1–7

> How lovely is your dwelling-place,
>   Lord Almighty!
> My soul yearns, even faints,
>   for the courts of the Lord;
> my heart and my flesh cry out
>   for the living God.
> Even the sparrow has found a home,
>   and the swallow a nest for herself,
>   where she may have her young –
> a place near your altar,
>   Lord Almighty, my King and my God.
> Blessed are those who dwell in your house;
>   they are ever praising you.
>
> Blessed are those whose strength is in you,
>   whose hearts are set on pilgrimage.
> As they pass through the Valley of Baka,
>   they make it a place of springs;
>   the autumn rains also cover it with pools.
> They go from strength to strength,
>   till each appears before God in Zion.

The place where the Lord lives is truly one of great peace. Here it is described as 'lovely' (v. 1), something to be yearned for (v. 2) and a place of praise (v. 4). The psalmist has realised that every human yearning for refreshment is met only in God. I'm expecting to come back from my holiday well-rested, but within a few weeks I know I'll be busy and stressed with life again unless I make time to spend with God, allowing him to still my rushed heart. When we are weary or desperate, it might be tempting to look to the leisure options that the world offers, but only God can truly restore us and provide lasting fulfilment.

The good news for us is that, since Jesus came to earth, died and rose again, we can have God living right inside of us. We don't need to journey to the temple to know God's presence very close; we can simply call out to him right where we are. Whether we are on holiday in a picturesque place, enjoying a slow pace of life or knee-deep in nappies and sleepless nights with endless jobs to do, God can fulfil and restore us and bring peace to our hearts.

Not only that, but God is with us in every stage of our lives. This psalm uses the metaphor of a pilgrimage to describe how God wants to bless us at every point on the journey. If you've ever felt that yearning feeling, that weariness to the point of fainting, described in verse 2, this is your reminder to allow God to strengthen you as you go from day to day. It is only in his strength that we find ourselves able to make the Valley of Baka (a dry, desolate place) a place of springs. If you're suffering at the moment – physically, mentally or just worn out from all the commitments your life entails – know that God can provide rich nourishment even in these times.

In a podcast I listened to earlier today, Olly Goldenberg said: 'Bumps are what we climb on.' None of us want 'bumps' in our life – we'd much prefer a smooth, even path where everything falls into place and nothing ever happens to cause anxiety. But imagine trying to climb a wall with no bumps to place your feet on or to grab hold of. It would be impossible! The bumps in our lives help us to climb further in our relationship with Jesus, until one day we'll see him face to face. This is why we can go from strength to strength, even as we pass through our 'Baka' – because we know that in everything God is shaping us, using our experiences to chip away at the rough edges of our characters and form us more into the likeness of his Son.

Prayer

- What is your 'Valley of Baka' at the moment? An area of suffering, uncertainty, difficulty or pain?

- Ask the Lord for an insight into what he's teaching you through this time. Wait for his response and note it down if you like. Pray into this, asking him to give you strength to make your hard time a 'place of springs', somewhere rich in blessings, even if they're not what you would have chosen.

Stillness idea

Visualise (or draw, if you like) two mountains, each called 'Strength'. In the middle is the Valley of Baka. Imagine yourself journeying with Jesus by your side, from Strength to Strength, going through Baka in between. What sustenance do you find in the valley? What unexpected blessings are there? What is Jesus saying to you? What is the expression on his face? Where is he and where are you?

Reflect

Remember that you don't need to wait till you're on holiday or have more time to enter the presence of the Lord. Ask him for strength as you go about your busy days, knowing that only he can refresh you even while you're still moving.

DAY 11

Be Still

— even when you're anxious about money.

Introduction

For those of us who worry about money, stillness can seem evasive. No day goes past that doesn't involve money in some way or other, and we can find ourselves constantly on edge about whether or not we're going to be able to afford to support our families, buy a house, cut our hours, pay into a pension fund or send our kids to university.

This twitchiness can really threaten our ability to be still before the Lord. It can throw us lies like 'God doesn't care about you' or 'God isn't able to provide for you'. It can cause us to doubt whether God is trustworthy – and, since a large part of being still involves trusting God with the things we can't control, this becomes a problem.

I won't say today's passage makes things instantly easier – shifting our mindset with regards to money is never an overnight process in my experience – but it certainly gives us a foundation to help us on our journey of being still when our financial status is uncertain.

Read 1 Timothy 6:6–10

> But godliness with contentment is great gain. For we brought nothing into the world, and we can take nothing out of it. But if we have food and clothing, we will be content with that. Those who want to get rich fall into temptation and a trap and into many foolish and harmful desires that plunge people into ruin and destruction. For the love of money is a root of all kinds of evil. Some people, eager for money, have wandered from the faith and pierced themselves with many griefs.

Our culture worships money and celebrates those who make it. If you run your own business, you will find your social media feed full of people promising a guaranteed way to make your first million, convert followers to clients, build a six-figure coaching business in just 15 hours a week or some other unrealistic claim. It seems that you've 'succeeded' in life if you've made money and 'failed' if you haven't.

This passage, however, flips that narrative upside down. Money is repeatedly spoken about negatively, while contentment is praised. The desire for money can trap us, leading us to crave things that are bad for us or might even destroy us (v. 9). Chasing money can bring huge grief into our lives (v. 10). Don't we know this from experience? We hear stories of people whose attempts to get rich have led to disgrace, shame, regret, fraud, bankruptcy, maybe even imprisonment. Perhaps we've had personal experience of the heartache that large amounts of money – or the pursuit of it – can bring.

But in a world that believes that to have money is to have it all, Paul is clear that true 'great gain' is actually *contentment* (v. 6). He reminds us that we can't take money with us when we die (v. 7) and that actually all we really need is something to eat and something to wear (v. 8). It makes perfect sense – and yet many of us struggle to live this out in our daily lives. Why?

Most of you will be reading this as reasonably well-off people in a reasonably well-off country. If you don't feel 'rich', please check out **givingwhatwecan.org**, entering your country, household income and number of household members. It will tell you how your wealth compares to everyone else's in the world. It's a simple tool – there are far more complexities to wealth than income, of course – but the sobering results make their point: it turns out that we have more than we think.

We are surrounded by wealth, comfort and apparent financial 'security'. We may have enough, but we crave more – not only because our sinful natures are naturally focused on ourselves, but because we see people all around us gaining 'more'. Paul talks about falling into temptation when it comes to chasing money, and he's not wrong. We're social creatures, hugely influenced by the people who are part of our lives. Daily we are tempted to want what they have.

I can't overestimate how hard it is to push back against our materialistic culture with the attitude Paul is describing here. But it is not impossible. And, in fact, it is essential if we are to experience the godly contentment that Paul entices us with. I think we can draw some practical help from his words:

- **Capture the vision (v. 6)** – the more we absorb verse 6 into our hearts, the more we will *want* to pursue godliness and contentment over money. We can write out this verse, repeat it to ourselves daily, ask God to make this our strongest desire – whatever it takes to set our eyes on this eternal goal.

- **Be grateful for what we have (v. 7)** – rather than bemoan that we don't have the kitchen extension or sports car that our neighbour has, we can be grateful that we enjoy clean water, plentiful food, a roof over our heads, education, healthcare… the list goes on. As we learn not to take these things for granted, we will realise just how much we have.

- **Desire Jesus (v. 10)** – if desiring money has the potential to make us 'wander from the faith', then desiring Jesus is the obvious antidote. Drawing closer to Jesus – even when we don't yet *feel* still or content – is an act of trust. We are trusting that the more we desire him, the more our desire for money will fade, and the easier we will find it to be still.

The world is continually dazzling us with shiny objects and promises of contentment, but it cannot deliver. Jesus is the only one who can cause us to be truly content with what we have, saving us from the destructive power of money. As we lean in to what Jesus is doing in our lives, what he has given us and what he is calling us to, we can trust that he will lead us, step by step, into a future for which he has already provided.

Prayer

- Consider in which area or areas of your life you find yourself tempted to desire money. It might be in home ownership or improvements, cars, gadgets, clothes, experiences or food.

- Ask God to draw close to you, filling you with contentment in this area and reducing your desire for whatever it is you crave.

Stillness idea

One way to counteract our cravings for contentment through money is by giving it away. Next time you find yourself craving something to fill a gap, buy it or pay for it and gift it to someone else. Whether it's a meal in a fancy restaurant, a beautiful vase, a clever new gadget, buy it (if you can afford it) and pray about who God wants to bless through it.

Reflect

How did this act of generosity make you feel? Was it harder or easier than expected? What was the response of the person you gave to? How did it answer a prayer or fill a need for them?

Be Still

— God's given you community.

Introduction

Who are the people around you, the ones who cheer you on in good times and bad? Perhaps your church small group comes to mind, your close friends, your parents, siblings, spouse or children.

God has not designed life to be lived in a bubble, but within community – which is good news for busy people, as it means that our desire to draw close to him is not something we have to accomplish on our own, without help. We may feel that the hectic pace of our lives makes peace and contentment elusive, but when we accept the help and support of others, we find that God can accomplish great things in our hearts – even when we're busy.

Read Exodus 17:8–13

> The Amalekites came and attacked the Israelites at Rephidim. Moses said to Joshua, 'Choose some of our men and go out to fight the Amalekites. Tomorrow I will stand on top of the hill with the staff of God in my hands.'
>
> So Joshua fought the Amalekites as Moses had ordered, and Moses, Aaron and Hur went to the top of the hill. As long as Moses held up his hands, the Israelites were winning, but whenever he lowered his hands, the Amalekites were winning. When Moses' hands grew tired, they took a stone and put it under him and he sat on it. Aaron and Hur held his hands up – one on one side, one on the other – so that his hands remained steady till sunset. So Joshua overcame the Amalekite army with the sword.

This story from the life of Moses is the epitome of what it means to support one another. Each one has their part to play. It is Joshua's job to choose who will defend the Israelites against the Amalekites. It is the job of the chosen soldiers to fight. It is the job of Moses to hold God's staff up high, praying for victory. And it is the job of Aaron and Hur to support him in doing so. Overall, however, it is God who will bring victory through all these people in their different roles.

In this passage, we learn the importance of committing our activities to God and praying for success, whatever that looks like. It's all too easy to forge ahead when busy and forget to seek God's will in what we're doing. Do you pray as you open your laptop, begin an interaction with a difficult person or visit a friend who's having a rough time? I know I'm often so distracted by the task in hand that I forget to bring God into it.

But in addition to this, God has put others in our lives for the purpose of supporting us and being part of what we are doing. Again, it's easy to forget this or play it down. We don't want to burden people, even those who love us dearly, so we don't ask for what we need or share our struggles vulnerably with them. Why share our hectic work schedule with our friends – don't they have their own work to be concerned with? Why share our overwhelming family life with our colleagues – it's not of interest to them, is it?

When we're honest with others about our struggles, we usually find that they're delighted to help. It gives them a sense of purpose, makes them feel valued by you and often deepens the relationship. Whether it's a friend taking your kids for an afternoon to help you focus on work, your church small group bringing round meals in a busy week or a work colleague offering to take some tasks off your plate, we do others a disservice when we don't allow them in to be part of what we are doing.

Making ourselves vulnerable like this doesn't come naturally to busy people, many of whom are high-functioning and – let's be honest – get a kick out of being able to spin a lot of different plates at once. We don't like admitting that perhaps we've bitten off a little more than we can chew. But what happens when we do? We bring ourselves out of the picture so that God's glory can be seen more clearly. What did the Lord say to Paul when he was struggling? 'My grace is sufficient for you, for my power is made perfect in weakness' (2 Corinthians 12:9).

Moses had performed miracles, bravely asked Pharaoh to let the Israelites go, brought ten plagues down on Egypt and eventually led God's people away from slavery and into freedom – with a whole load of problems along the way. We consider him to be one of the heroes of the faith. And yet here he is, unable to hold his arms up high for hours on end, because it turns out he's only human. It was God's power – not Moses' strength – that would bring the Israelites victory on this occasion.

Rather than people looking at us and marvelling at our inner strength, our resilience, our activity, our busyness, as we admit we can't do it all, that we are tired, weary or running out of time to meet a deadline, we are able to point to God, joining with Paul in saying, 'When I am weak, then I am strong' (2 Corinthians 12:10). And others will see that we are not super-human – but that we trust in a super God.

Prayer

- Is there anything you're involved with right now where you need help? Are your closest friends and family members aware of your current level of busyness and how you're coping with it?

- Pour out your stresses to God. Share with him what you need. Ask him to provide people to help, and allow him to point you towards individuals who could partner with you. Ask him to help you be vulnerable before others.

Stillness idea

To write this book, I knew I had to take some annual leave and get away for a couple of days. The intentional slots I'd booked into my calendar to work on it just weren't happening: work, children and other projects quickly seeped into these allotted times. So I asked my husband whether he could juggle things at home for a couple of days, found some time in the calendar which looked free, booked an Airbnb and went for it. This won't be the solution for everyone, but is there something you're doing right now where you can call on the help of others? Rather than try to juggle everything simultaneously, can you book some time out to focus on one particular responsibility? Who would need to be involved?

Reflect

How have you been able to cope better due to the help of others? How do you think this may have changed your approach to future times of busyness? Will you call on others again?

Be Still

— you don't need to do it all.

Introduction

I wonder if you've ever thought about the source of your busyness?

I don't mean the responsibilities and commitments that make us busy, but rather the mindset that leads to a busy life. While we can blame our busyness on having lots to do, the truth is that some of us seem to be more wired towards a busy lifestyle than others. I've often pondered whether my busyness is a good thing or a bad thing. If God has given us a high capacity for juggling different parts of life, then surely he is to be praised for that. But if our non-stop pace has more to do with lies we've believed about ourselves or our place in the world, then perhaps we need to bring these out into the open and lay them before God.

I'll warn you: this can be a painful process. It often involves looking into our past for messages we may have absorbed at different times which have led to our crazy-paced lives now. It might mean we realise ways in which our parents or others have – deliberately or inadvertently – contributed to the unsustainable lives we live now. Where this is discovered to be the case, God brings us the phenomenal gift of forgiveness. Through Jesus' work on the cross, we are given the power to forgive those who have hurt us. We are all works in progress, shaped by the good and the bad things we've experienced in life. By God's grace, we can be shaped more by his Holy Spirit than by our negative experiences.

Read Psalm 131

> My heart is not proud, Lord,
>   my eyes are not haughty;
> I do not concern myself with great matters
>   or things too wonderful for me.
> But I have calmed and quietened myself,
>   I am like a weaned child with its mother;
>   like a weaned child I am content.
> Israel, put your hope in the Lord
>   both now and forevermore.

This short psalm packs a punch. David understands something common to so many of us: the desire to plan, organise and control. Whether it's a government hoping to eradicate poverty, a group of climate protesters hoping to save the planet or a young adult trying to map out the rest of their life, God has placed in us the mental capability and desire to work for change in our lives and world.

It's a good desire – in its rightful place. It leads a government to change policies to benefit the most vulnerable. It leads climate protesters to reduce their carbon emissions and encourage others to do so. It leads a young adult to make sensible decisions about their finances. But our human power is finite. There is only so much we can do before we have to give the rest over to God. We don't know which new social crisis is around the corner for the government. We're not exactly sure which actions will guarantee our planet's future. And a young adult has no idea what might happen to their health or those around them as their life unfolds.

This psalm is an acknowledgement of our limitations. It is not an excuse to do nothing – remember, David was a king. He'd have been pretty busy with a bunch of high-level initiatives. But he was still able to give them over to God enough to say, 'I do not concern myself with great matters or things too wonderful for me' (v. 1). He did what he could, then he gave the rest over to God.

Sometimes the source of our busyness is a feeling that if we don't do this, it won't get done. No one will pick it up. Someone will try to take over, but they won't be as good at it as we are. These are embarrassing beliefs to admit about ourselves, but we only need admit them to God – and are reassured that 'there is now no condemnation for those who are in Christ Jesus' (Romans 8:1).

When we try to be wholly responsible for something, without acknowledging God's activity in our lives, it leads to exhaustion and illness. One of my former vicars told me about a time his youth workers were burnt out. His direction to them was to stop the youth work – a brave move in a church with lots of teenagers, including his own kids. One year later, fresh leaders came forward to volunteer. They'd seen the need for youth work and responded to God's call to help.

My vicar took this psalm to heart. We heard about this story, which happened long before we arrived in the church, but also saw the same attitude in his leadership as we worshipped and worked under his leadership. God was God, and we were not. The well-being of this vicar's flock was more important to him than the ministries they led. He trusted that God was working in the lives of his congregants, and that it was a privilege – not a necessity – for us to join in. He was able to calm and quieten himself. As busy people, are we learning to do likewise?

None of us are indispensable to God's plans. God, in his generosity, has given us a desire and capacity to do what we do – but he also gives us wisdom over when to stop, to rest, to lay things aside for a season or longer. Then we can say with David 'like a weaned child I am content' (v. 2).

Prayer

- Consider your responsibilities (make a list if it helps). Is there anything where you're in danger of believing success hangs solely on you? Anything which is burning you out and needs to be laid aside, but you're worried that no one else will pick it up?

- Take your honesty to God. Acknowledge where you have relied on your own strength and not his. Sense the relief of unburdening your commitments on to him (1 Peter 5:7).

Stillness idea

Write down a list of all your responsibilities. Include people and animals you care for, paid work, church involvement, community volunteering, key friends and family who regularly make up part of your week.

Then, taking each item on your list separately (you could do this over a few days if you wished), ask God what he wants to say to you about each one. Spend one or two minutes in silence, expecting God to communicate – he might pop a key Bible verse into your head, a reassuring phrase about that responsibility or a relevant picture or idea. Jot down next to each responsibility what God has said about it. This act of taking the detail of our lives to God is humbling, reminding ourselves that he is Lord over all we do.

Reflect

What is God saying to you about your busy life? Where is he affirming, strengthening and comforting you? Where is he asking you to pull back?

Be Still

— you don't need to do it all at once.

Introduction

Some of my own busy mindset stems from the fact that life is so full of fun opportunities. I don't want to miss anything! I want to grab them with both hands and teach my kids to do the same, because who knows how long we have on this earth? I certainly don't want to be regretting missed moments on my death bed.

Yet we don't need to be doing everything at once. Most opportunities will come round again. Some don't, of course, so we need God's wisdom to discern what to say 'yes' to right now, but other events, roles, activities or responsibilities will do. And if they don't? Perhaps it was never meant for us. We are finite humans, limited by our time and energy levels. The aim is not to do it all, all at once, but to ascertain what God has for us in this current season.

Read Ecclesiastes 3:1–13

There is a time for everything,
    and a season for every activity under the heavens:
        a time to be born and a time to die,
    a time to plant and a time to uproot,
    a time to kill and a time to heal,
    a time to tear down and a time to build,
    a time to weep and a time to laugh,
    a time to mourn and a time to dance,
    a time to scatter stones and a time to gather them,
    a time to embrace and a time to refrain from embracing,
    a time to search and a time to give up,
    a time to keep and a time to throw away,
    a time to tear and a time to mend,
    a time to be silent and a time to speak,
    a time to love and a time to hate,
    a time for war and a time for peace.

What do workers gain from their toil? I have seen the burden God has laid on the human race. He has made everything beautiful in its time. He has also set eternity in the human heart; yet no one can fathom what God has done from beginning to end. I know that there is nothing better for people than to be happy and to do good while they live. That each of them may eat and drink, and find satisfaction in all their toil – this is the gift of God.

If you ever feel a sense of guilt that you've had to turn down a request for help or disappointment that you're not involved in something you'd have loved to do, this passage holds encouragement for you. 'There is a time for everything', it begins, and we immediately get a sense of a God who is not burdening us with more stuff to do, but who is ordering and balancing our lives. Rather than running around like headless chickens, seizing every opportunity that comes our way,

God is giving us the gift of being discerning, measured and wise about what we take on and when.

When my oldest child was a few months old, I returned to worship leading at my church. It was something I'd done lots of prior to motherhood, and it was a way to serve that I enjoyed. But with a church leader husband also involved in the service, it took a lot of complicated arranging to make it work, and eventually I knew that it wasn't the right decision for my baby boy.

This was confirmed by a picture a good friend had for me. I was in a pear orchard and picked two pears: one I ate there and then, the other I put in my pocket for later. It was such a distinct and odd picture I knew it was from the Lord, and as I prayed about it, I realised God was saying that worship leading was the pear I needed to put away for later. That reassurance that I was not saying 'no' for good, but for a season, gave me a lot of peace as I handed in my notice and focused instead on setting up a group to serve babies and toddlers through the service. Sure enough, when God led us to a new church a few years later, what did they need more of? Worship leaders! Our children were old enough that we could make it work between us.

Seeing our life as made up of different seasons is a gift to busy people, but also a challenge. We cannot sustain a life made up of incessant hurry, but we can sustain a season of it. When things are particularly hard to juggle, the question is: is there an end in sight? If so, how will we mark this, ensuring that the next season isn't as frenetic? If not, what needs to change? Is there a responsibility or commitment that God is calling us to lay down, to enable us to know some of the stillness he brings?

Verses 9–13 are a reminder to us all that the work we do – whether paid or unpaid – should bring us satisfaction. It is easy for us, when over-busy, to resent our work, our voluntary commitments or even the demands our family bring, but God has created us to work. This might be our paid job, caring for family members, serving at church, volunteering in the community or a combination of all of those. If we are starting to resent them, perhaps that is a nudge from God that we are trying to live lots of seasons at the same time.

God has 'set eternity in the human heart' (v. 11). We are made to be in communion with God forever. There will be time to enjoy all sorts of things, in this life and in our eternal life in heaven. We don't have to do it all at once. One day, the earthly frustrations of our lives will vanish – but the journey of getting to know our heavenly Father starts right now, amid those frustrations. We do not need to wait to learn to be still in God's presence.

Prayer

- Consider whether you are currently in a busy season, a quiet season, or whether there is simply no end in sight to what you are experiencing right now.

- Ask God to map out your week/month/year as appropriate, showing you where he wants you to commit your energy, and where he might be asking you to step back. If you're in a busy season, ask him how to ensure that it actually stops at the end and offers some respite, rather than moving on to more busyness.

Stillness idea

We have four seasons in a year. Actually, in the UK, we frequently have four seasons in a day! They are marked by different temperatures, amounts of rain and length of day. This passage says there is 'a season for every activity under the heavens' (v. 1). Using paper and pens, map out what the next year or so looks like for you. Are there defined seasons where you know you will be busier? Opportunities for quieter weeks/months? You could use different colours to denote different seasons. This activity may help you become more aware of the opportunities for rest, and thus more keen to protect them.

Reflect

How does your year look? How has it helped to do this exercise? Are there any decisions you'll be making because of what you have mapped out?

Be Still

— the Lord is enough.

Introduction

Busy people love being busy. They usually have high capacity, but also a high zest for life, which leads to them taking up every opportunity open to them, squeezing their calendars to see how much more they can fit in, almost like it's an Olympic sport. I know this because I am one of them. So if you're nodding your head reading this, you're not alone! And busy people tend to attract busyness, because others see that you're coping and ask you to do more. The old adage 'If you want something done, ask a busy person' is, sadly, true.

We often think busyness itself is the problem. I've come to see, though, that this isn't true. Busy people can be a great gift to their families, their workplaces and their church, because they can deal with having a lot on their plate, juggling different responsibilities with organised efficiency.

What we need to be aware of is not the danger of being busy, but the motivation behind our busyness. If we are caught in the rat race because we're desperately trying to prove ourselves or fulfil ourselves, that's a warning sign. God has proven himself to us over and over again, and is the only one who can fulfil us. Our identity as his children is the most valuable label we will ever receive, so if we suspect that our busyness may be an attempt to gain others' approval or fill a hole in our lives, we will need to unpick it if we want to learn what it means to be still.

Read Lamentations 3:22–26

> Because of the Lord's great love we are not consumed,
>   for his compassions never fail.
> They are new every morning;
>   great is your faithfulness.
> I say to myself, 'The Lord is my portion;
>   therefore I will wait for him.'
> The Lord is good to those whose hope is in him,
>   to the one who seeks him;
> it is good to wait quietly
>   for the salvation of the Lord.

In this passage, we are encouraged to be still in the words 'wait for him' (v. 24) and 'wait quietly' (v. 26). This isn't a hollow command, an act of blind faith to a God who may or may not show up. Both verses come *after* a declaration of who God is. We are told of his love, his mercy, his compassion (v. 22), his daily faithfulness to us (v. 23) and his goodness (v. 25). It is *because* of these things, therefore, that we can trust him, that we can wait for him to fulfil the salvation he has promised us. The writer would have been waiting for the Messiah. We have gratefully received him, his death and resurrection, but are still waiting for Jesus' return, when all will be put right forever.

These verses, comforting as they are, contain a challenge to us busy people. It is all too easy – I know from experience – to rely on our own strength to get through the day and our own achievements to see us through life. Many of us busy people are competent plate-spinners and high-achievers. Even if we're trying to rely on God's strength, it's common to slip into self-sufficiency. So how do we do it? How do we fix our eyes on the Lord as we go about our busy days? Four truths from this passage stand out to me:

- **'We are not consumed'** (v. 22) – it is helpful and healthy to daily remind ourselves that, were it not for God's love and mercy, we would have no hope for the future and might not even be here today. However much we can achieve in our own strength, we cannot achieve our own eternal destiny – and so we always have a reason to turn to God in gratitude for this.

- **'His compassions... are new every morning'** (vv. 22–23) – as we have seen in previous devotions, God provides us with what we need each day. Daily acknowledging his hand in our lives gives us that regular excuse to turn our eyes towards what he is providing, not what we have accomplished.

- **'The Lord is my portion'** (v. 24) – everything we need is found in God, not only our fulfilment, but our purpose and identity. And he gives us everything we need to complete the tasks before us. We don't need to strive for anything, because we have what we need right here. It has already been provided for us, and we don't need to earn it. Out of this truth, we are free to engage in, and enjoy, meaningful work which glorifies God.

- **'The Lord is good to those whose hope is in him'** (v. 25) – when we experience success, to whom do we attribute it? Whether it's the end of a project, the conclusion of a role or a breakthrough in a relationship, we can use these moments to turn our eyes once more to the Lord, praising him for his goodness to us.

We can enjoy the many activities and roles God has given us when our faces are tilted towards him, praising him for his love and waiting for Jesus to come again to make our salvation complete.

Prayer

- Be honest with God: where does your motivation lie? When you say 'yes' to a new commitment, what is the underlying reason? And what is your attitude as you undergo it?

- Reread these verses as a prayer, using them as a declaration of what you know to be true about God. Supplement them, if you like, with your honest feelings about these lines – which ones you're struggling to live out right now, and which ones bring you great peace and comfort as you say them.

Stillness idea

It is easy, when busy, to rush manically from one activity to the next. As you go about your day today or tomorrow, deliberately slow down in a task or two. Whether it's taking extra time to do a household chore or sitting down and making eye contact with a family member, rather than having a rushed conversation on the go, be intentional about remembering that God has given you everything you need. Your salvation does not depend on whether you complete your to-do list.

Reflect

How easy do you find it to slow down and wait? What is the impact when you do this? Are you more or less productive, or does your productivity stay the same? What could you implement to ensure that your day includes frequent reminders to turn to God and acknowledge his goodness?

Day 16

Be Still
— let God provide.

Introduction

I wonder how much of our busyness arises from what we think we need to provide for ourselves. Whether we're working hard to pay the bills and stay out of debt, taking on extra work in hope of a promotion or volunteering lots so that people will think well of us, it's hard to fully trust that God knows what we need and wants to give it to us. I know this from experience. Much as we may have heard the familiar words of today's reading many times, it can feel impossible to actually live like we know them to be true.

However, if we want to learn how to be still before God even when we're busy, then absorbing the unfailing steadfastness of God will be an essential part of this. How does this happen?

Read Matthew 7:7-12

> 'Ask and it will be given to you; seek and you will find; knock and the door will be opened to you. For everyone who asks receives; the one who seeks finds; and to the one who knocks, the door will be opened.
>
> 'Which of you, if your son asks for bread, will give him a stone? Or if he asks for a fish, will give him a snake? If you, then, though you are evil, know how to give good gifts to your children, how much more will your Father in heaven give good gifts to those who ask him! So in everything, do to others what you would have them do to you, for this sums up the Law and the Prophets.'

It's easy to develop a lot of anxiety around the things we perceive we need but that we don't yet have. Sometimes it's a material item – a car, a spare room, a designer outfit, an overseas holiday, a new phone or better insurance. But it might just as easily be a character trait – better social skills, more energy, less anger or a kinder heart. Our cravings can make us twitchy, impatient, working harder in our own strength to try to force these things to come to us. But the dissatisfaction we feel with our lot in life is the very opposite of what it means to 'be still'.

We need to find a way to trust God with the things we long for. The language here is very simple: ask and you'll receive, seek and you'll find, knock and the door will open. But God's schedule is not ours, and his infinitely wise knowledge of what we need is (fortunately) not the same as ours. It is rare – in my experience – to receive something immediately after praying for it. And this can cause us to try to gain it for ourselves. Remember Abram and Sarai? They had to wait over a decade for God to provide the son he'd promised for them. I'm not surprised they got sick of waiting after a few years and decided to take matters into their own hands – yet the sombre end to that story (Genesis 16, 21) reminds us that forging ahead with our own plans for provision is never a good idea.

Trusting God to provide what we need brings us a deep measure of stillness, but it's not easy in the real world. What principles can we gain from this passage?

- **We get what we need, not necessarily what we want.** While the language in verses 7–8 is direct, it's also deliberately vague. When we ask, 'it' gets given to us. When we seek, we will find… what, exactly? And when we knock, the door will be opened – but with no sense of what we might find behind it. When we leave our needs with God, we may not have them met in the way we are expecting.

- **God does not make mistakes with what he gives us.** He is our perfect, heavenly Father. But again, there is vagueness. If our child asks for bread, we will not give them a stone – but we won't necessarily give them bread either, if we don't deem it to be in their best interests. The point here is that when we ask for something good, we will not receive harm. We can trust God to give us the right thing for our situation.

At the end of 2022, I was fed up and on the verge of burnout, working for myself. I asked God what I should do: either give up my business or find more hours in the day to work harder at it, in the hope of gaining more success with it. He provided neither option, but instead offered a third option: a maternity cover in a job which suited my skillset perfectly, would provide a steady income and would offer a chance to reflect on where my business was going. I'm so glad he didn't give me either of the options I asked for. I couldn't see an alternative, but, as my loving heavenly Father, he could. Like a Christmas present which you weren't expecting but is perfect in every way, God generously gave me the surprise gift of a beautiful job.

It is not always easy to trust God, but I'm encouraged that it is a journey. We don't need to do anything drastic, but as we trust him in the small things and see that he provides over and over again, we gain faith to trust him for bigger and bigger things. I am convinced that as we entrust the deepest desires of our heart to the Lord, he can do miracles in our lives. Providing what we've asked for is only a small part of the story. There's a whole lot more he wants to do in our hearts and with our characters through the process of longing and waiting. We ask, and we receive – many times more than we were expecting.

Prayer

- What is it that you long for the most in life at the moment? What unsettles you or keeps you up at night?

- Ask God to provide this for you. If it's helpful, you could visualise yourself handing it over to him in a box. You can trust that he will not give you the wrong thing or a bad thing. You can also be assured that, however long it takes for God to provide in this situation, he will be teaching you and shaping you as you wait.

Stillness idea

Asking God for our deepest desires is rarely an overnight process. It can involve weeks, months or even years of asking, but knowing that he is able to provide good things, and that he is providing other important things in the waiting, can help us to trust him when it's hard. If there is something you particularly desire at the moment, it might be helpful to start each day handing over this desire to him. Ask him for what you want. It may not be given if it is not in your best interests – but God will always show up and do something miraculous in our hearts when we bring our needs before him.

Reflect

After a few days of asking, reflect on how your heart has changed. Are your prayers different? Has your 'ask' changed in any way? Has God taught you anything through the asking?

Be Still

— receive God's good gifts.

Introduction

Sometimes it feels as if our culture deals only in the big. 'Go big or go home' seems to be the prevailing phrase. Everything must be lived to the max. You work hard; you play hard. What once was considered a luxury is now a necessity. Days out, weekend breaks, holidays are amplified.

But this can create unhealthy patterns of keeping going for far too long without a break, holding out for that next all-inclusive holiday or five-star weekend away. God has designed us to live with regular moments of rest and sustenance, and when we are busy, we can easily forget the importance of the daily mercies God provides.

Read 1 Kings 19:1–9

Now Ahab told Jezebel everything Elijah had done and how he had killed all the prophets with the sword. So Jezebel sent a messenger to Elijah to say, 'May the gods deal with me, be it ever so severely, if by this time tomorrow I do not make your life like that of one of them.'

Elijah was afraid and ran for his life. When he came to Beersheba in Judah, he left his servant there, while he himself went a day's journey into the wilderness. He came to a broom bush, sat down under it and prayed that he might die. 'I have had enough, Lord,' he said. 'Take my life; I am no better than my ancestors.' Then he lay down under the bush and fell asleep.

All at once an angel touched him and said, 'Get up and eat.' He looked around, and there by his head was some bread baked over hot coals, and a jar of water. He ate and drank and then lay down again.

The angel of the Lord came back a second time and touched him and said, 'Get up and eat, for the journey is too much for you.' So he got up and ate and drank. Strengthened by that food, he travelled for forty days and forty nights until he reached Horeb, the mountain of God. There he went into a cave and spent the night.

I'm going to go out on a limb here and assume that you're not currently being hunted down by a crazy queen. But I think there are aspects of Elijah's mood here that we can all identify with. He's been doing the Lord's will, he's seen miraculous intervention – and yet still he finds himself in a place of danger. We are pressing on with what we believe the Lord has called us into – but may be feeling just as weary or afraid as Elijah.

What does God do? He grants Elijah sleep and food: two basic human necessities that we need every day. They don't make the situation any better – Queen Jezebel still wants to kill Elijah – but they give him what he needs to face it. Well-rested and well-fed, he has the strength to make a long journey to a place of safety (vv. 8–9).

This passage reassures me because often I don't feel that I could easily become much less 'busy'. Sure, there are commitments I could lay aside, and I could get better at saying 'no', as well as planning out my diary a little better so that big projects didn't overlap in the way they seem to. But even without these adjustments, I still have four kids and a job. I have a home and garden to care for, family and friends to support, a church family to be part of. Life is just always going to be a certain level of busy. And I'm guessing that if you're reading this, you may be in a similar situation, with little potential to stop being busy altogether.

Our culture says work, work, work till you can't do it anymore, then go on the most lavish holiday you can find. No matter if you can't afford it – buy now, pay later! Our phones don't help: we are bombarded with constant forms of entertainment, 24/7. There is always information being thrown at us from every angle, music to listen to, people to keep up with, plans to make. It takes discipline to be able to switch off.

In a culture that harangues us till we're worn out, then charges us to go on a holiday we can't afford in order to recover, God refreshingly says: 'Don't neglect the simple daily gifts I'm giving you.' When we are exhausted like Elijah, we can accept small pockets of rest and refreshment in our day: a simple meal, eaten away from our screens; a short walk in the fresh air; a proper night's sleep rather than staying up to fruitlessly toil away at something or other.

No matter that it's not a three-week cruise or a visit to the Turkish baths: God can take those few minutes of stillness in our lives and multiply their impact considerably. When we allow him to minister to us using the simplicity of daily necessities, we do indeed find capacity to be still in even the busiest, most exhausting times of life.

Prayer

- Do you find yourself living towards the next holiday or break? What are the daily opportunities for rest God is giving you?

- Ask God to open your eyes to see where he is daily sustaining you in simple ways. Thank him for all the ways he does this, and ask him to help you make the most of even short times of stillness and refreshing.

Stillness idea

Find a few minutes today when you can be still and soak up God's goodness during something you're already doing. It could be taking the dog for a walk and choosing not to cram your ears full of music or podcasts but simply to take in the beauty and stillness around you. It could be a moment with a friend or family member where you put your phone in another room and choose to be fully present with them. It could even be a trip to the bathroom on your own (parents of young kids, you know what I'm talking about).

Reflect

How was this brief moment of stillness? What did it mean to you to be able to be present, enjoy your surroundings and give your mind a chance to be still? God gives us these gifts every day: will we be bold enough to ignore the distractions and take them?

DAY 18

Be Still
— it is God's gift to you.

Introduction

Our passage today is a common one, and you may have heard it many times before. I wonder if, like me, you've tended to gloss over it in the past, believing it to be not true or relevant in your own life because what Jesus is promising doesn't seem like a reality right now?

2 Timothy 3:16 says: 'All Scripture is God-breathed and is useful for teaching, rebuking, correcting and training in righteousness.' There is no part of the Bible that isn't relevant or useful to us at some point in our lives – including when it comes to rest. God's word in the following verses is as much for us who feel burdened by our busyness as it is for anyone.

Read Matthew 11:25-30

> At that time Jesus said, 'I praise you, Father, Lord of heaven and earth, because you have hidden these things from the wise and learned, and revealed them to little children. Yes, Father, for this is what you were pleased to do.
>
> 'All things have been committed to me by my Father. No one knows the Son except the Father, and no one knows the Father except the Son and those to whom the Son chooses to reveal him.
>
> 'Come to me, all you who are weary and burdened, and I will give you rest. Take my yoke upon you and learn from me, for I am gentle and humble in heart, and you will find rest for your souls. For my yoke is easy and my burden is light.'

Rest – ah! The thought of it is tantalising – particularly when our lives are rushed and hectic. We long for a time when we can stop, breathe deeply and feel at peace again. We push ourselves to breaking point in advance of a holiday, anticipating that this is when 'rest' will come and restore us.

I wonder, though, whether in absorbing this definition of 'rest' we have, in fact, absorbed a worldly view of what it means. To the world, rest is something that happens when we're not working – which, for those who feel like they're constantly working, feels unattainable. Jesus' definition is broader. He's not saying that rest *can't* be a stopping of work – we regularly read of times when he himself rested in this way, taking himself off to spend time with his Father or relaxing at a meal with friends – but that it is not *just* a stopping of work.

Look at verse 29 – it is in taking Jesus' yoke upon us and learning from his gentle, humble way of doing life, that we will find rest. It is right to have times when we stop completely – observing a weekly sabbath, having some time off every few months, going on holiday to replenish our energy levels. But Jesus is inviting us into a *way of life* that is restful. Even when we are working, our souls find rest. Why? Because instead of carrying our own burdens, we carry Jesus' burden. The burden of putting God first and living as a disciple of Christ is far, far easier and more restful than the burdens of achieving the next big thing or surviving a season of non-stop activity.

Being still has a combination of aspects to it. Sometimes it is physical stillness, but often it is a peace within our busyness, a tilting towards God's face even as we feel like we're drowning in stuff to do, a trusting of God even as we are overwhelmed by what's ahead of us. In this passage, Jesus is showing us the possibility of a life characterised by rest and stillness, not because we are inactive, but because our activity is from him – and it is light and it is easy. He is effectively swapping our burdens for his, taking the stress and strain of our daily lives and replacing them with an eternal perspective, where we can keep the things of this life in proportion to what is waiting for us in heaven.

I love that Jesus precedes this idea by sharing how the wisdom of God's kingdom has been revealed to little children (v. 25). When you watch children go about their lives, what is it that characterises their actions? It is an unburdened lightness that comes from having total faith in those around them to provide what they need. Most children don't have to burden themselves with where the next meal is coming from or whether they'll have clothes to wear tomorrow. They trust that the adults in their lives will do their job, so they can play and enjoy the freedom of knowing they are provided for.

As an adoptive parent, I'm all too aware that some children don't enjoy this freedom. They have to take on burdens beyond their years, because those who should be providing for them aren't doing so. I wonder whether sometimes we treat God as an uncaring parent, not able to do his job in caring for us. We take on burdens we were never meant to have, because God is actually full of love and care and more than able to provide for us.

Of course, this doesn't mean we sit around doing nothing and expect him to rain money down on us, but it does mean that we actively take on his burden, following his leading into the right opportunities and trusting that he will take the heavier burdens away from us.

Prayer

- What is your attitude to 'rest'? Is it something you work towards or something you incorporate into everyday life?

- Talk to God about rest and how you feel about it. Tell Jesus what you feel about his yoke – is it something you're prepared to take on or do you need a bit more clarification about what it entails? Ask him to show you what it looks like in your life right now.

Stillness idea

Choose one thing you have to do today. How will you approach it restfully? What are your burdens regarding this one thing – can you actively give them over to Jesus? What is the burden he is replacing it with – does it feel lighter? Undergo the activity with intentionality, being mindful of carrying Jesus' lighter yoke as you do so.

Reflect

How did the activity go? Will you try this again next time you do the same job? Could you bring this attitude into other parts of your life?

Be Still

– observe the sabbath.

Introduction

I have never been in a conversation or Bible study about the sabbath in which we didn't get ourselves tangled up in knots. It's such a complicated issue! In my current life-stage of raising children, it can be difficult to know what 'work' is and therefore what should be avoided. After all, I cannot stop caring for my children on the sabbath, even though I might consider some aspects of that to be 'work'. We may choose to have friends round for a meal on the sabbath, which takes a lot of preparation and hard work. And of course we may be serving – or even leading – at church, which is also work.

Yet we know that the concept of having one rest day each week is a sound one. God has ordained it because he has designed our bodies and minds to need that amount of rest. It is a pattern he set out in creation – six days of work, one day of rest – even though he himself does not need rest. When we observe the sabbath, we are by default slowing down and learning to be still before our creator.

Read Matthew 12:1–13

At that time Jesus went through the cornfields on the Sabbath. His disciples were hungry and began to pick some ears of corn and eat them. When the Pharisees saw this, they said to him, 'Look! Your disciples are doing what is unlawful on the Sabbath.'

He answered, 'Haven't you read what David did when he and his companions were hungry? He entered the house of God, and he and his companions ate the consecrated bread – which was not lawful for them to do, but only for the priests. Or haven't you read in the Law that the priests on Sabbath duty in the temple desecrate the Sabbath and yet are innocent? I tell you that something greater than the temple is here. If you had known what these words mean, "I desire mercy, not sacrifice," you would not have condemned the innocent. For the Son of Man is Lord of the Sabbath.'

Going on from that place, he went into their synagogue, and a man with a shrivelled hand was there. Looking for a reason to bring charges against Jesus, they asked him, 'Is it lawful to heal on the Sabbath?'

He said to them, 'If any of you has a sheep and it falls into a pit on the Sabbath, will you not take hold of it and lift it out? How much more valuable is a person than a sheep! Therefore it is lawful to do good on the Sabbath.'

Then he said to the man, 'Stretch out your hand.' So he stretched it out and it was completely restored, just as sound as the other.

In this account from Matthew, Jesus does two things which the Pharisees consider to be unlawful, according to the Old Testament teaching on the sabbath. One is allowing his hungry disciples to pick and eat grain on the sabbath – note Jesus himself does not eat. The other is healing a man's shrivelled hand, restoring it completely, in the synagogue. We'll look at each one in turn.

In Exodus 16, we read of the Israelites collecting manna in the desert (see more on day 7). God provided enough so that the day before the sabbath, they could collect double, ensuring that they would not have to work on the sabbath itself. The manna stayed good to eat all the way through the sabbath. This principle of preparing food before the sabbath was probably what was in the Pharisees' mind as they observed what the disciples were doing. How dare they put their own physical needs before God!

But the context was entirely different. The Israelites were being provided for on a regular, day-to-day basis. God made it very clear where each meal was coming from, and when. The disciples, however, lived hand to mouth, accepting whatever food was offered to them by others. They did not have money or their own home, but instead went from town to town accepting the hospitality of others. I can well imagine that they may not have eaten for days at this point. And their hunger matters to God. In Mark's retelling of the same incident, he adds, 'The Sabbath was made for man, not man for the Sabbath' (Mark 2:27). Jesus is permitting his disciples to be fed and provided for on the sabbath, just like the Israelites were fed and David and his men were fed. The Pharisees saw the sabbath as a restrictive law, a way of getting others in trouble; Jesus communicated that it was God's gift to us: a freedom, a permission.

Then Jesus enters the synagogue and sees the man with a shrivelled hand. The Pharisees predict what he is about to do, so try to catch him out again using the sabbath as a weapon. But Jesus' response (v. 11) reminds them that even they wouldn't hesitate to do something good – even if it was considered 'work' – on a sabbath. They would rescue their sheep from a pit and – as Jesus comments in a similar incident recorded in Luke – they would rescue their child from a well (Luke 14:5).

What do these incidents teach us busy people about what we can and can't do on the sabbath? First, we do not need to succumb to legalism surrounding the sabbath, which is God's gift of rest to all of us – even those of us who feel we cannot stop. If our busy lives mean we can't prepare food ahead of time or need to put on a laundry load on the sabbath, we shouldn't beat ourselves up about it. But second, the sabbath is the Lord's day. It is a day for looking around us and seeing what good we can do in the world – even if that sometimes feels like hard work. As we glorify God by resting from at least some of our usual work and fixing our eyes on him, he will bring stillness to our hearts, placing us in a good position to work the week ahead.

Prayer

- Do you have a defined 'sabbath'? Is it Sunday or another day? How do you ensure it is set apart for the Lord?

- Ask the Lord to help you understand and enjoy the sabbath more. Ask him to bring to mind ways in which tasks or schedules could be rearranged, to allow more space for him.

Stillness idea

Consider how your sabbath is usually spent. Is it restful? Is it focused on the Lord? Are there jobs you regularly do on the sabbath which could be done in advance or saved till the following day? Are there restful, leisurely activities you could schedule in, to make yourself stop and rest? Try this out for a few weeks!

Reflect

After a few weeks, reflect on how the sabbath has been. Have you noticed a difference? Do you feel more rested, more still, more free? Is there something else which could change – a routine, a schedule or even a heart attitude – in order to enjoy the sabbath more?

Be Still
— do not conform.

Introduction

Our world is not still. We are called to be still in a world which hurries and rushes and pursues and chases and overwhelms and exhausts. It can feel tiring just to try to push against that culture.

But fortunately our desire to be still is not simply a pleasant platitude or shareable meme to live by, with no ultimate goal. Neither is it something we do in our own strength. As Christians, we have the power of the Holy Spirit living inside us to help us become more like Christ. And we have an eternal hope for which we are living, a motivation for the sometimes painful work of moulding our sinful beings into the glorious people God created us to be. One day Jesus will be revealed to all the world, renewing heaven and earth, and calling us to live in God's presence, with no more suffering, forever.

Read 1 Peter 1:13–16

> Therefore, with minds that are alert and fully sober, set your hope on the grace to be brought to you when Jesus Christ is revealed at his coming. As obedient children, do not conform to the evil desires you had when you lived in ignorance. But just as he who called you is holy, so be holy in all you do; for it is written: 'Be holy, because I am holy.'

I think often our struggle with being still arises from it being the complete opposite of the world we live in. Whether we're talking about physical, mental or emotional stillness, we don't see a lot of it around us. Instead we see a striving – to become rich, to pursue goals, to work hard, to find fulfilment in relationships, to travel the world, to buy a dream home – a striving that never stops at its stated goal, because that goal will never achieve contentment for the one who strives.

So we can see the sense of Peter urging us to 'not conform to the evil desires you had when you lived in ignorance' (v. 14). We might think of 'evil' as doing bad things – but really it is any desire that's not in line with God's will, any desire which puts our own needs above God's perfect plan for us. The key to stillness is to refuse to live life as the world lives it, to refuse to conform to desires which don't put God first.

Easier said than done? Peter has some guidance for us. First, we are to remain alert and sober (v. 13). This doesn't necessarily refer to alcohol (although if drink is becoming something we rely on regularly, we will need to address this with God and with professional organisations who can help). The heart of this verse is raising our awareness that the world doesn't preach the same as Jesus does and to be discerning in how we process what it tells us. We can so easily get sucked in, so Peter is reminding us to be on our guard. Just because those in your workplace, family or social group are living a frazzled, on-edge life doesn't mean you have to.

Second, Peter calls us to frame our lives with an eternal perspective. Keeping our eyes fixed on Jesus' return (v. 13) helps us to see the other aspects of our life in the right proportions. It is not unimportant to do a good job at work, but it isn't the end of the world if we don't get promoted.

Third, he calls us to be holy (v. 15). We find the original directive in Leviticus 11, just after a whole bunch of laws regarding clean and unclean food. Holiness here is set within the context of keeping all the laws God has given, in regards to being set apart from the world. But because Jesus came to fulfil the law, these outer rules are no longer necessary. Jesus has become holiness for us, and we get to take on his holiness through believing and accepting that his death and resurrection won these things for us. So when Peter calls us to be holy, he's not expecting us to do that in our own strength; he's encouraging us to believe and accept Jesus as our Saviour and commit to the ongoing work of the Holy Spirit in our lives.

Attempting to be still in an unstill world can feel like climbing Everest, but we do half the work when we acknowledge the very different cultures of earth and heaven. We live in the world but do not belong to it (John 15:19). Understanding that we're running a different race can free us up to make decisions that others might question, because we know that to find true stillness, we need to draw closer to the one who provides it, the one who has bought our holiness.

Prayer

- Where do you feel you are often most tempted to do as the world does and not as you believe Jesus might have you do? (If you're not sure, spend some time asking God to reveal this area of your life to you and waiting for his response.)

- Invite Jesus to minister to you in this area. Ask him to give you an obedient heart and ultimately to make you more like him.

Stillness idea

Lots of songs and hymns have been written around the theme of holiness. Play one of them now. Find a space where you won't be interrupted, close your eyes and enjoy listening to the words as you contemplate God's holiness and that, through Jesus, he is making you holy too.

Reflect

If this has been a helpful practice, plan some other times when you could sit and listen to a worship song without doing something else at the same time.

Be Still

— know your limits.

Introduction

I don't know whether you work outside the home, or used to, and in what capacity. Often busy people are those who attract responsibility within the workplace, because they are good at managing a large number of different projects and people. Your job may, at times, have been a stressor for you, and you might have found yourself asking, *How did I end up in this position? I'd like to have a bit less responsibility*. Being in charge of a team or a project can be fulfilling, but also daunting.

Today's reading reminds us that the buck doesn't ultimately stop with us, however much responsibility we have in work or in wider life. God is in control, and we can rest in his sovereign care, knowing that it is he who looks after the universe and cares deeply for us.

Today's reading holds a similar sentiment: do what is required, but don't absorb responsibility which isn't yours – leave it to God.

Read 1 Peter 5:6–11

> Humble yourselves, therefore, under God's mighty hand, that he may lift you up in due time. Cast all your anxiety on him because he cares for you.
>
> Be alert and of sober mind. Your enemy the devil prowls around like a roaring lion looking for someone to devour. Resist him, standing firm in the faith, because you know that the family of believers throughout the world is undergoing the same kind of sufferings.
>
> And the God of all grace, who called you to his eternal glory in Christ, after you have suffered a little while, will himself restore you and make you strong, firm and steadfast. To him be the power forever and ever. Amen.

One of the things which can contribute to a busy mind is worrying about things we can't control. But just as a teacher is not expected to lead a school or a retail employee is not expected to lead the marketing team at head office, so we are not expected by God to do any more than we have power to do. So what *is* in our power?

- **We can humble ourselves** (v. 6), recognising that we are not ultimately in control of our lives, the planet and human history, but that God is sovereign over all and mighty to act. When we do this…

- **We can cast all anxiety on to God** (v. 7). Nothing we go through is too big or too small for God to be listening to, concerned for and able to not only reduce our anxiety but to work out the issue in question in a glorious way, when we bring it before him. And part of the journey of this is that…

- **We can be alert and sober** (v. 8), with open eyes and ears to see and hear what God is doing with the things we are anxious about, how he is working out solutions, what he is saying to us about them and how he is changing our heart through the process. And when we do this…

- **We can resist the devil** (v. 9), confident that others have stood firm too. Although it might feel like we are alone as Christians when we look at the world, the reality is that we are not alone. Millions of people through history, and all over the world today, have trusted in Jesus' resurrection, finding hope for eternity. Many have suffered to the point of persecution or even death because of their faith in Jesus. This can give us confidence when we're feeling weak in ours.

So these are the things we can do – our '9–5' if you like. But God is the master CEO – all power and responsibility lies with him. This passage also tells us what he is able to do.

- **He is mighty to lift us up** (v. 6) when we lower ourselves before him. It's counter-intuitive, but it works. If you want to be great, humble yourself and let God lift you up to where you were designed to be – not where you think you should be. It will be far, far better than where you could have got to by yourself because…

- **He cares for us** (v. 7). God cares about every individual detail of our personalities and the lives we live. He *knows* every individual detail better than even we do, because he created us this way! So we can trust that when we put our lives and our stresses into his hands, he will do the most amazing things, and ultimately…

- **He will bring us to eternal glory** (v. 10). Keeping this perspective of whose we are and where we are going and how this all ultimately ends can genuinely help us to put daily stresses and strains in their rightful place. God works in our heart to shift our mindset, but he doesn't leave us to scrabble about here on earth either, because as we put our lives in his hands we find that…

- **He can restore us** (v. 10), giving us strength to carry out what he has called us to do – in our family, workplace, church and community.

When we are able to live within our limits as finite, flawed humans, submitting our lives to God, we will start to see the signs of his power as he works through the things which worry or concern us. And as God works, we can be still.

Prayer

- Read through the eight **bold** points above again. Which one is a sticking point for you, something you find hard to do yourself or to believe about God?

- Bring this before God now, asking him for strength to believe and live this truth.

Stillness idea

Find a place where you won't be disturbed for a few minutes. Think of a commitment or relationship going on in your life right now which is causing you worry or stress. Set a timer for five minutes, or whatever you can manage, and bring the truth of God's word to this situation. Repeat the point you highlighted in the prayer section above, say it over and over, read it, ask God how you can live it for this situation and listen for what he is saying to you. Practise being still.

Reflect

How do you feel after this short time? How has God changed your perspective on this situation or encouraged you in it? Jot down anything you want to remember.

Be Still

— receive the joy of the Lord.

Introduction

Looking around at those we work with, live with or send our kids to school with, it doesn't take long to realise that many people are burdened by all sorts of worries and fears. Life is hard. And with no place to take our shame and guilt, we turn in on ourselves.

The Bible, as always, is good news for those of who are hurting and broken. Jesus has beaten death, eliminating its power over us forever. He has paid the price for our sin, meaning that we don't need to beat ourselves up over our mistakes or live in shame. There is nothing God cannot forgive us for, nothing he cannot restore, no area of life to which he cannot bring the great joy of knowing we have a Saviour and a guaranteed eternity with him – forever.

Read Nehemiah 8:2–12

So on the first day of the seventh month Ezra the priest brought the Law before the assembly, which was made up of men and women and all who were able to understand. He read it aloud from daybreak till noon as he faced the square before the Water Gate in the presence of the men, women and others who could understand. And all the people listened attentively to the Book of the Law.

Ezra the teacher of the Law stood on a high wooden platform built for the occasion. Beside him on his right stood Mattithiah, Shema, Anaiah, Uriah, Hilkiah and Maaseiah; and on his left were Pedaiah, Mishael, Malkijah, Hashum, Hashbaddanah, Zechariah and Meshullam.

Ezra opened the book. All the people could see him because he was standing above them; and as he opened it, the people all stood up. Ezra praised the Lord, the great God; and all the people lifted their hands and responded, 'Amen! Amen!' Then they bowed down and worshipped the Lord with their faces to the ground.

The Levites – Jeshua, Bani, Sherebiah, Jamin, Akkub, Shabbethai, Hodiah, Maaseiah, Kelita, Azariah, Jozabad, Hanan and Pelaiah – instructed the people in the Law while the people were standing there. They read from the Book of the Law of God, making it clear and giving the meaning so that the people understood what was being read.

Then Nehemiah the governor, Ezra the priest and teacher of the Law, and the Levites who were instructing the people said to them all, 'This day is holy to the Lord your God. Do not mourn or weep.' For all the people had been weeping as they listened to the words of the Law.

Nehemiah said, 'Go and enjoy choice food and sweet drinks, and send some to those who have nothing prepared. This day is holy to our Lord. Do not grieve, for the joy of the Lord is your strength.'

> **The Levites calmed all the people, saying, 'Be still, for this is a holy day. Do not grieve.'**
>
> **Then all the people went away to eat and drink, to send portions of food and to celebrate with great joy, because they now understood the words that had been made known to them.**

After 50 years in exile in Babylon, some of the Israelites have returned to Jerusalem. Ezra and the Levites spend several hours ('from daybreak till noon', v. 3) publicly reading God's law to the people and explaining it so they can understand more about who God is and how he interacts with them. It should be joyful, God-focused time – but instead the people start to weep. You cannot listen to the law without also being aware of your own lawlessness.

It must have been quite a scene: a large crowd of God's people so racked with guilt for what they had done and who they had been and who God was that they were publicly and noisily crying. Into this chaos, the Levites calm them, saying, 'Be still.' In this context, the word used for 'still' suggests a literal quietness, a holding of the peace. They are effectively saying, 'Don't cry, it's okay – God wants to give you his joy to sustain you. There will be a time for confession, but right now we're going to celebrate God.'

The chapter which follows tells the story of the Israelites' repentance. It involves fasting and sackcloth and elaborate speeches. When Jesus came, he did away with lengthy, ritualistic confession. When we sin, we have the incredible privilege of being able to turn to God directly, thanks to Jesus' death and glorious resurrection, to repent and seek forgiveness.

What does this have to say to busy people? When life is full, we can easily be distracted from the ways we have hurt others and hurt God. It can feel simpler just to press on as normal with our manic lives, throwing ourselves from one activity to another. But the underlying guilt and shame we experience when we don't expose our sin to our heavenly Father can cause more stress and overwhelm. It can add to the things we are already doing and make them ten times harder because our minds are distracted and weighed down by the burden of what we have done.

It is good news that we have a Saviour in whose presence we don't need to be ashamed. It is phenomenal that we have forgiveness available to us through the cross. We don't need to feel worried that we won't be able to cope with exposed sin – whether ours or other people's – because 'the joy of the Lord is your strength' (v. 10). Don't put off any longer sharing the hidden, hurting parts of your life with the God who loves you and longs to heal.

Prayer

- Are there any broken relationships, hidden sins or hurtful situations that you're trying to hide in order to concentrate on your busy life – but which you know are weighing you down?

- Bring these to Jesus now. Be honest with him. There may be tears – that's okay, the Israelites cried too! Then spend some time listening to what he might be saying. Is there an action you need to take? Some painful situations are not instantly fixed overnight – even though we can trust that God's forgiveness is immediate and eternal. You may need to continue to bring the situation before him for days, weeks or months to come, as you process and learn to forgive others.

Stillness idea

Each time you find yourself getting distracted by a painful situation, instead of trying to sweep your emotions away, make space for them. Make a point of sitting with how you feel – either at the time or at a later point that same day – identifying what you're feeling and asking why you may be feeling like that. Extend the compassion to yourself that Jesus does.

Reflect

Are you someone who deals with sin (your own and other people's) honestly and directly? Or do you try to force down the hurt and carry on with life as normal? How could 'the joy of the Lord is your strength' alter your perspective?

DAY 23

Be Still
— you don't need to be afraid.

Introduction

Fear is a very real emotion permeating our society right now. Within a relatively short space of time, we have been faced with a worldwide pandemic, a housing shortage, a cost-of-living crisis and very real concerns over climate change and our deteriorating planet. The availability of huge amounts of news (and fake news) via our smartphones, as well as the unattainable lifestyle standards presented to us via social media, are leading to soaring levels of anxiety among the younger generation.

I often wonder whether being a Christian makes much of a difference to our minds and our hearts as we inhabit this uncertain world. For sure, we are not immune to mental ill health any more than we are immune to physical ill health. But today's passage seems to suggest that we can have a peace and a stillness despite what's going on around us. The words of Jesus 2,000 years ago are as relevant today as they've ever been.

Read John 14:23–27

> Jesus replied, 'Anyone who loves me will obey my teaching. My Father will love them, and we will come to them and make our home with them. Anyone who does not love me will not obey my teaching. These words you hear are not my own; they belong to the Father who sent me.
>
> 'All this I have spoken while still with you. But the Advocate, the Holy Spirit, whom the Father will send in my name, will teach you all things and will remind you of everything I have said to you. Peace I leave with you; my peace I give you. I do not give to you as the world gives. Do not let your hearts be troubled and do not be afraid.'

As busy people, there are many things in life which stress us out. Aside from the national and international concerns above, we can find ourselves frazzled by juggling a seemingly impossible calendar of appointments, commitments and deadlines. It's no wonder that many of us feel anxious or fearful about what we have to do, who we have to meet and what they will think of us.

But none of this comes as a surprise to God: 'Well our feeble frame he knows', as the hymn says. And he also knows well the complicated and hurting world we live in. He made us and he made it; there's nothing he doesn't already know or understand about how his creation operates. So when he encourages his disciples not to be troubled or afraid, it isn't some kind of hollow platitude. He really does know that *despite* our frailty and *despite* the world's darkness, it is still possible to relinquish fear. Why?

The answer comes in verse 27. Jesus has gifted us his peace. And it's not the same type of peace, nor the same method of giving, that we get from the world. Our culture says peace can only come when you've stolen a moment of quiet away from the rabble of your family or when you've booked time off in a gorgeous resort – and even then peace is temporary and external. By contrast, the peace Jesus gives 'transcends all understanding' (Philippians 4:7). It lasts forever and it permeates deep into the core of our beings. It guards our hearts and minds from the stressful, ungodly influences around us.

The good news for busy people is that because this peace is internal, we can know it even when externally we're rushing around, juggling diaries or feeling the pressure at work. Physical stillness is helpful, yes, but it's not a prerequisite for having hearts and minds that can be still before the Lord. What is required, according to Jesus' words here, is that we love God (v. 23) and stay open to the Holy Spirit (v. 26) in our lives.

We may still experience anxiety and worry to varying degrees. Our bodies and minds are not perfect, and healing does not always come this side of heaven. But the difference we have, as children of the living God, is the underlying peace of knowing that, one day, all the trouble we experience here on earth will come to an end, and God's perfect kingdom of love and justice will reign forever. This knowledge helps put our busy days into perspective and reminds us that our minds can know peace, even when our lives are hectic.

Prayer

- What causes you most anxiety right now? Is it a worldwide issue, like climate change, a national problem, like overcrowded prisons, or a personal situation in your family or work life?

- Ask Jesus to come and bring his peace, even as you're concerned for these things. Ask him to open your heart to the work of the Holy Spirit as you learn to lean into peace over worry.

Stillness idea

Reread today's Bible passage slowly. Bring to mind the things which trouble your heart and bring fear. Picture yourself putting them into a box and handing them to Jesus. Ask him what he wants to give you instead. Jot down anything you sense him saying to you in this time.

Reflect

How is Jesus meeting you in your fear right now? What is he saying? What are you finding difficult or challenging, and how is he responding? How will you respond back? Make a note of anything significant.

DAY 24

Be Still

– in a world that is not.

Introduction

It is not wrong to be busy, but sometimes there is a heart attitude at the core of our busyness which *is* wrong. For me, it is a need to find my identity through achievement. I need to constantly check my motivation for taking on *yet more things* and ask myself who I'm doing this for and why.

This isn't easy, though, when the world around us values the things that God does not. The world says you are valuable because of what you do, how much you earn, how well your children turn out, the places you frequent or the clothes you wear. Pushing against this – particularly when we are people whose characters naturally turn themselves towards a busy schedule – can feel impossible. Today's reading encourages us.

Read Romans 12:1-3

> Therefore, I urge you, brothers and sisters, in view of God's mercy, to offer your bodies as a living sacrifice, holy and pleasing to God – this is your true and proper worship. Do not conform to the pattern of this world, but be transformed by the renewing of your mind. Then you will be able to test and approve what God's will is – his good, pleasing and perfect will.
>
> For by the grace given me I say to every one of you: do not think of yourself more highly than you ought, but rather think of yourself with sober judgement, in accordance with the faith God has distributed to each of you.

I love how Paul's communication style here has been translated as 'urging' us – clearly for the people of first-century Rome, conforming to the world was every bit as much of a temptation as it is for us now. Paul knew how difficult it would be for those reading his words to live them out, which is why he emphasises their importance.

And they *are* important. This is surely the central truth of what it means to be a Christian: we are no longer living for the world, but for God. Our bodies are his (v. 1) and our minds are his (v. 2). It is all for God. Every decision we make must be taken with the truth of God's word in our hearts. Every life-junction we get to must cause our eyes to lift to heaven and ask: **What's next, Lord? What would you have me do here? Where should I go?**

It's easier said than done, though, isn't it? We are living in the world. We are living in a society which doesn't put God first, which decides for itself how to use its money, which seeks to better itself year on year, which does what feels good. And the results, to us, look tempting and often without risk.

Paul's words 'Do not conform to the pattern of this world' probably need to be stuck up over my bed so that I can read them each morning, because every day I am faced with questions and decisions and turning points, big or small, to which I must ask myself: **Am I going to conform to the world or seek God's will in this?**

When it comes to our diaries and the question of which new commitments or activities to take on, this passage gives us several questions to ask:

- **Is this an opportunity to sacrifice something for God? My time, money, status?** (v. 1)
- **Is this God's will? Do I sense him leading me into this?** (v. 2)
- **Am I tempted by this only because it will lead to higher status, more money or affirmation from those around me?** (v. 3)

I believe it also has something to say to those of us who lead lives which are busy with things we can't easily say 'no' to (e.g. caring for children or elderly relatives, paid work, an illness which eats our time). It both encourages and challenges us:

- **Even when others don't see my efforts, God is pleased by them. Am I fulfilling my duties begrudgingly or feeling his pleasure as I sacrifice myself in worship to him?**
- **I might not be doing what others of my age or stage are doing, but I am living according to God's good, pleasing and perfect will. Am I allowing him to renew my mind in this season?**
- **As I humble myself and serve others, God is glorified through what I do. Am I finding contentment in the faith God has given me?**

I have a good degree from a good university. For the first few years of my career, all looked promising: I was climbing the career ladder of education and carving a name for myself. But God had also given me a strong desire to stay at home with our children, so when I became pregnant, this is what I did. 'What a waste!' said a GP to me, when she discovered I wasn't planning to return to teaching yet. When I returned to my (Christian) secondary school for a reunion concert, the retiring head teacher, who had been my head teacher, looked visibly disappointed when I told her what I was doing with my life. I'd been one of her star students, full of A-grades and Oxbridge-bound when we'd last met, and now I was 'just' at home, looking after my children.

This is not about whether it's 'godlier' to stay at home with your children or go back to work. I have seen Christian families do a variety of things when it comes to work and childcare, and many of them have been successful. But for me and my family, I do believe this is how God was renewing our minds, calling us to not automatically conform to how the world does things. And it turns out there was good reason. After two children, God called us to adopt two more. Adopted children come with trauma, and it turned out to be significant that I was at home to give them the attachment and regulation time they needed. My experiences of parenting went into a blog, which became a small business and ministry. I don't believe any of this would have happened had I gone back to work immediately.

And guess what? After 15 years out of the classroom, I've now returned to teaching. God has worked my life out, not in a way I ever expected, but in a way which has brought much joy and peace to our family. My time at home with our children was not a 'waste', as my GP thought, nor was it a disappointment, as my head teacher thought, but part of God's perfect plan to be glorified through my gifts and life-stage.

Don't be conformed to how the world thinks about things, but in everything you do allow God to transform your mind. He will do something extraordinarily good when we make ourselves still before him.

Prayer

- Return to the questions and encouragements in **bold** above. Which one stands out to you?

- Talk it through with God now.

Stillness idea

Look back at your life. Can you think of a time you allowed God to renew your mind and not conform to what those around you were doing – and how it worked out? Bring it to memory and thank God for what he taught you in that time.

Reflect

Is 'not conforming… but being transformed' a part of your discipleship right now? Is it something which used to happen but has slipped? Or something that has never really happened? How can you take small steps to allow God in to transform your mind? You won't regret it!

DAY 25

Be Still

– relinquish control.

Introduction

'If you want something done right, do it yourself.' This saying makes me more than a little uncomfortable – largely because I believe it, but wish I didn't.

Delegating tasks to others doesn't come easy to many of us. We might have a set idea of how we want something done, feel that it would take longer to explain the task than just do it ourselves, or perhaps have had a bad experience of entrusting a task to someone who let us down. But a key aspect of being still before the Lord is the ability to relinquish control over what there is to be done. Much as I find my husband's method of hanging laundry totally baffling, I have to admit that it's not a matter of eternal significance – but that doesn't mean I always find it easy to share out the jobs or lay them aside when necessary. Today's reading, at its heart, is about whether we are ready to hand over control to Jesus and let him direct our lives.

Read Luke 10:38–42

> As Jesus and his disciples were on their way, he came to a village where a woman named Martha opened her home to him. She had a sister called Mary, who sat at the Lord's feet listening to what he said. But Martha was distracted by all the preparations that had to be made. She came to him and asked, 'Lord, don't you care that my sister has left me to do the work by myself? Tell her to help me!'
>
> 'Martha, Martha,' the Lord answered, 'you are worried and upset about many things, but few things are needed – or indeed only one. Mary has chosen what is better, and it will not be taken away from her.'

I think many of us can relate to Martha. My house is no show home, but there are still things I strive to have in place by the time guests show up: a tidy lounge with space for people to sit, a table already laid and the food preparation underway, so that I can enjoy spending time with those who have come to visit. If I'm running behind schedule or our guests are early, I definitely feel the pressure. So I sympathise with Martha here, who just wants to make things lovely for such a special visitor.

But Jesus challenges her about her heart attitude towards him. I love the gentle way he does this, with compassion flooding out of him as he gets right to how she's feeling: 'You are worried and upset about many things' (v. 41). He's not harsh or condemnatory – he sees that she wants to welcome him, but she is just going about it in the wrong way. Martha is trying to make the environment perfect for welcoming Jesus, but Jesus doesn't need us to be neat, tidy, prepared or perfect before we can sit and listen to him. He just needs us to come to him as we are, with open hearts and minds, ready to learn from, and be changed by, him.

Martha is holding on to some elements of control, while Mary is relinquishing control in the presence of Jesus. There is security in doing what we've always done, following the same routines and rituals, and Martha is doing what she knows best: preparing to welcome a very special guest to the home she shares with her siblings. And yet this guest is different: he requires that she lays down what she knows, puts her security in his hands and focuses on the 'one thing' that is needed – to be in the Lord's presence, listening and learning.

As a busy person, I tend to prioritise tasks over spending time with the Lord. Perhaps you do too. Obviously, there are things we need to get done during the day – few of us can live monk-like existences of uninterrupted hours of prayer and communion with Jesus. But there is a stillness which comes when we make even a few moments with him a priority to our days. There is a peace which comes from being able to say: 'Lord Jesus, I hand over my day, my tasks and my busyness to you.' There is a relief when, like Mary, we can relinquish control, inviting God to have his way in our lives.

Even in the busiest of seasons, even when the jobs haven't been completed, even when we don't feel 'ready', Jesus is calling us to come, sit at his feet and learn from the rabbi. When we do, we find our hectic calendars become more ordered, priorities emerge more clearly and our perspective aligns more with God's. We are works in progress, for sure, but no minute we spend with Jesus will ever be wasted. Our to-do lists are always full, and completed jobs will always need doing again eventually (I'm looking at you, laundry bin). But when we pause to listen to Jesus, the eternal benefits are never in vain.

I wonder what happened after this passage; we only hear a fragment of the story, after all. Did Martha go and sit with Mary? For how long? Did they eat that day, and, if so, who prepared the meal if they were both listening to Jesus? I like to think that they both listened to Jesus (we see Martha's deepened faith in John 11), and then, somehow, the meal got made and they enjoyed eating together. But how much richer were they at the end of the day because they had learnt to relinquish control, prioritising Jesus over the very many things they had to do.

Prayer

- Are there areas of your life in which you struggle to relinquish control? Are there people you could delegate things to? Or tasks which you know are not important but struggle to let go of?

- If you are able, lay these things before Jesus now. Confess how you have wanted to be in control of your life and ask him to take the lead instead. If this feels a step too far, ask Jesus to help you relinquish control where you feel stuck and unable to right now.

Stillness idea

Try this creative prayer exercise. Go to a room where you're unlikely to be disturbed and close your eyes. (You can either read through these instructions then do the exercise from memory or read them out loud slowly while you record them onto your phone, playing them back to guide you through what to do.)

Imagine you are in Mary and Martha's home. What does it look like? What can you smell? Which room is Jesus in and how is it laid out? Imagine yourself going to sit at his feet. Where and how are you sat? What is he saying? Are others talking too? What questions do you have for him? How do you feel when he looks directly at you? What is he saying to you?

Reflect

What did Jesus say to you? What did you say to him? Jot down anything significant in a journal or on your phone.

Be Still

— the Lord is active.

Introduction

When we are very busy, it's easy to get our priorities muddled. The big, important thing in life becomes whichever big, important thing is most obviously in front of us: tomorrow's work presentation; Saturday's church fun day; a busy week of getting our children to the right places at the right times in the right outfits for end-of-term events. Once we get through this, we tell ourselves, life will be easier, and we will turn our eyes to God again.

In my experience, though, this usually doesn't happen. Getting one thing out of the way only clears the path for another thing, then another, then another. Life doesn't seem to stop when you have multiple commitments and activities. So how do we shift this perspective and get our priorities back into their rightful place?

Read Zechariah 2

> Then I looked up, and there before me was a man with a measuring line in his hand. I asked, 'Where are you going?'
>
> He answered me, 'To measure Jerusalem, to find out how wide and how long it is.'
>
> While the angel who was speaking to me was leaving, another angel came to meet him and said to him: 'Run, tell that young man, "Jerusalem will be a city without walls because of the great number of people and animals in it. And I myself will be a wall of fire around it," declares the Lord, "and I will be its glory within."
>
> 'Come! Come! Flee from the land of the north,' declares the Lord, 'for I have scattered you to the four winds of heaven,' declares the Lord.
>
> 'Come, Zion! Escape, you who live in Daughter Babylon!' For this is what the Lord Almighty says: 'After the Glorious One has sent me against the nations that have plundered you – for whoever touches you touches the apple of his eye – I will surely raise my hand against them so that their slaves will plunder them. Then you will know that the Lord Almighty has sent me.
>
> 'Shout and be glad, Daughter Zion. For I am coming, and I will live among you,' declares the Lord. 'Many nations will be joined with the Lord in that day and will become my people. I will live among you and you will know that the Lord Almighty has sent me to you. The Lord will inherit Judah as his portion in the holy land and will again choose Jerusalem. Be still before the Lord, all mankind, because he has roused himself from his holy dwelling.'

Zechariah is full of interesting prophetic visions. We will look at one today and another tomorrow. In this vision, Jerusalem is being 'measured' to see whether it is ready to receive the fullness of God's kingdom. God is warning of the destruction of those who try to hurt his people, and encouraging them that he himself will one day come and live among them (vv. 10–11), but are they ready for him?

The question for us today, in the post-Messianic age, might be slightly different, but is just as important for us to consider: are we ready to receive Jesus in our hearts and our lives? I don't mean are we ready to become Christians. I'm assuming that if you're reading this, you probably already identify as one. But the decision to accept Jesus, to accept his gospel of grace, forgiveness and freedom, is one we are confronted with every day. Will we let Jesus into our work? Our finances? Our family? Our identity? Will we involve him in our decision-making, seeking to step into the purposes and plans he has for us? Will we give him our *all* or just our *some*?

Following Jesus is a lifelong journey of saying 'yes' to him over and over again. You might be aware of times you've said 'no' to him in the past – when you thought he was calling you to something you didn't want to do or when you ignored him because you knew what he would say and you didn't want to hear it. But this doesn't matter: God's grace is abundant when we bring our hearts to him. What matters is going forward: are we going to be busy people who say 'yes' to God before we say 'yes' to more busyness?

I was feeling overwhelmed with the responsibilities I had racked up when I attended a women's teaching day at a local church a few years ago. Two ladies prayed and prophesied over me. One of the pictures I was given was of tight ballet shoes being unwound from my feet. Once they were off, I could dance freely. It was not as technically perfect as it had been with the shoes on, but it was more expressive and joyful. God spoke to me powerfully through this picture, showing me one responsibility which I needed to lay aside. Once he said that, it seemed so obvious to me that I wondered why I hadn't thought of it myself. The answer, of course, is that I am not God! We might think we know what is best for us, but when we take it before God, he does wonderful things we would never have considered on our own.

This vision given to Zechariah ends with a command: 'Be still… because he has roused himself from his holy dwelling' (v. 13). Jesus has left his heavenly throne and come down to live among us, giving us an example to follow and a God who understands. We can be still, because God has been (and is still being) active. We can trust that he is working for our good constantly, and has been since before we were born. When we take every facet of our lives to him, he will direct us down the right path, giving us everything we need for the journey. And as we do so, we find our faith deepen, our ability to trust him grows and our sense of stillness – even within busyness – becomes more tangible.

Prayer

- Reflect on what God has done in sending Jesus. Are you ready to receive him every day, to allow him into every part of your life? Do you trust he will take you down the right path, or are you tempted to do what you think is best?

- Ask God to work within what you have going on right now. Stay open to what he might be saying to you about it.

Stillness idea

Find a quiet place where you won't be disturbed (you may have to plan this for some point in the future!). Set a timer for seven minutes. Ask God to speak to you. That's it! Stay still and quiet, and listen for the ideas, words, verse, pictures and emotions he brings to you. If you're questioning what you're hearing, ask God to take all other voices away so that you only hear his – then trust that what you're hearing is his. After the time is up, jot down what you remember. Please take care to weigh what you have heard, checking it lines up with scripture and perhaps asking a Christian friend to pray into this for you. God usually confirms his words several times, particularly if they are directional, so you can relax and wait for him to do this.

Reflect

How did you find this process of waiting on God? The creator of the universe is active in your life – how does that make you feel?

Be Still

— take small steps.

Introduction

It can be easy to feel overwhelmed by the enormity of what we have to do. Right now, I have a big project going on at work – finishing it by the deadline seems impossible. I'm writing this book – the deadlines are challenging. I have a large party to organise – with little idea when the planning is going to happen.

What God has been showing me in this season is that he knows what's going on in my life, and he has what I need to make it happen. Rather than procrastinate or become immobilised by the hugeness of what lies ahead, my job is to faithfully plod on each day, doing what I have capacity for and trusting in faith that he will do the rest. Amazingly, as I have done this, God has stepped in to do the miraculous: providing extra bits of time I wasn't expecting, accelerating my work over and above what I was expecting to achieve, and bringing in extra people to do things I thought I'd have to do.

Read Zechariah 4:1–10

> Then the angel who talked with me returned and woke me up, like someone awakened from sleep. He asked me, 'What do you see?'
>
> I answered, 'I see a solid gold lampstand with a bowl at the top and seven lamps on it, with seven channels to the lamps. Also there are two olive trees by it, one on the right of the bowl and the other on its left.'
>
> I asked the angel who talked with me, 'What are these, my lord?'
>
> He answered, 'Do you not know what these are?'
>
> 'No, my lord,' I replied.
>
> So he said to me, 'This is the word of the Lord to Zerubbabel: "Not by might nor by power, but by my Spirit," says the Lord Almighty.
>
> 'What are you, mighty mountain? Before Zerubbabel you will become level ground. Then he will bring out the capstone to shouts of "God bless it! God bless it!"'
>
> Then the word of the Lord came to me: 'The hands of Zerubbabel have laid the foundation of this temple; his hands will also complete it. Then you will know that the Lord Almighty has sent me to you.
>
> 'Who dares despise the day of small things, since the seven eyes of the Lord that range throughout the earth will rejoice when they see the chosen capstone in the hand of Zerubbabel?'

Again, we have another bizarrely fascinating vision which God has given Zechariah. The Lord is continuing to speak about the coming of his kingdom – what it will look like and how it will happen. With so much warfare up till this point in their history, the Israelites would be forgiven for believing that God's promised Messiah would show up with a sword and shield, ready to do battle with those who opposed God. We know that even when Jesus did show up in frailty and humility, many didn't recognise him because they still expected him to be a powerful warrior, prepared to lead an army. But here God says no, that's not the way that his kingdom will come. 'Not by might nor by power, but by my Spirit' (v. 6) is how he will conquer sin and death forever.

As busy people, it is easy to rely on our own might and power. It feels counterintuitive to stop and wait for God's Spirit to intervene, largely because God's timing never seems to be the same as ours and we're rushing to meet a deadline. But it's worth remembering that God's Spirit has done the most important thing in the whole of history: enabled God's kingdom to come. We must not, therefore, underestimate the importance of allowing God's Spirit to work in the – by comparison – far smaller and less significant tasks we must accomplish from day to day.

Verse 10 comes as an encouragement to us as we begin to hand our days over to the Holy Spirit: 'Who dares despise the day of small things?' asks the Lord. Good, important, significant things have to start somewhere. In the gospels, Jesus describes the kingdom of heaven as a sprinkling of yeast and a mustard seed. The key is to get the foundation right. Here, God speaks of a 'chosen capstone': Jesus. A capstone is not very big, but its quality and positioning are key to the ultimate success of the building it supports.

So when we have something big to accomplish, rather than becoming overwhelmed by its size or rushing to get it set up in the wrong way, we can be encouraged in the small steps we take each day towards its completion.

The mountain you're facing may not be a finite project with a deadline. It may be an ongoing issue, like knowing how to parent your teenager well, investing in a marriage which is struggling or wanting to be a valuable trustee to a charity. But the response is the same: submit your work to the Lord's timing – acknowledging that it may not be the same as yours – and, as you do so, trust that he will give you the right, small steps to take, ensuring that whatever the outcome, his kingdom is promoted and his name glorified.

Prayer

- Is there an area of your life that has become like an undefeatable giant recently? A mountain which seems impossible to move?

- Take this area to God right now. Ask him to guide you towards the right small steps and ask him for time and focus to work on these.

Stillness idea

I sometimes find it helpful to break down a larger project into smaller, manageable steps. As you take your 'mountain' to God, why not draw up a list, table or other visual image to help you see clearly what needs to happen within it? Chat to God as you draw and write. You may find it easier to take the small steps once you can see them written down – and it will act as an aide memoire on days when you feel distracted and unable to focus.

Reflect

How was this exercise for you? Has it helped to clarify, streamline and still your thoughts? In what ways do you sense God's stillness and presence with you as you faithfully work your way through the small steps?

Day 28

Be Still
— adopt God's priorities.

Introduction

Learning to 'be still' – even when we're physically *un-still* – is a mindset shift. Much of this devotional has been focused on how we shift our mindsets by turning our eyes towards God and seeking his perspective, his priorities.

I think we all know, deep down, that this is the key to true stillness in this life – but it's hard to stay faithful and unswerving when all around us are living with different goals. I know from experience that it's all too easy to get sucked into the worries and stresses of the world, all of which threaten to distract us from the gift of stillness God wants to give us.

Read Luke 12:13-21

> Someone in the crowd said to him, 'Teacher, tell my brother to divide the inheritance with me.'
>
> Jesus replied, 'Man, who appointed me a judge or an arbiter between you?' Then he said to them, 'Watch out! Be on your guard against all kinds of greed; life does not consist in an abundance of possessions.'
>
> And he told them this parable: 'The ground of a certain rich man yielded an abundant harvest. He thought to himself, "What shall I do? I have no place to store my crops."
>
> 'Then he said, "This is what I'll do. I will tear down my barns and build bigger ones, and there I will store my surplus grain. And I'll say to myself, 'You have plenty of grain laid up for many years. Take life easy; eat, drink and be merry.'"
>
> 'But God said to him, "You fool! This very night your life will be demanded from you. Then who will get what you have prepared for yourself?"
>
> 'This is how it will be with whoever stores up things for themselves but is not rich towards God.'

Jesus has been asked by one of his listeners to essentially play referee between him and his brother. As someone who spends many hours trying to keep the peace between twin boys, I don't know if it's reassuring or depressing to read that sibling rivalry is alive and well in adults too.

This particular brother wants Jesus to settle a dispute over inheritance. Of course, Jesus can't do this – it's not his family, and he's sensibly not getting involved – but what he does do is use the situation as a springboard for talking about greed. Instantly, Jesus has detected what is at the heart of this man's request: a desire for worldly wealth. Perhaps this feels a bit harsh – after all, the brother is only asking for what, presumably, is rightfully his. Wouldn't many of us feel hard done by if our parents' inheritance went only to a sibling and not to us as well? The question, perhaps, is why he wants the money and what he's planning to do with it.

To illustrate his point, Jesus tells a parable about a man who builds more and more *unnecessary* wealth. We're not talking about a man who worked hard to provide for his family and pay the bills. We're talking about a man who already has more than enough (verse 16 states that he was already rich, and then enjoyed an 'abundant harvest'). This is a man who already has everything he needs and more, so he has no need for his additional wealth. What does he decide to do with his surplus? Store it up for a future he does not know. In fact, Jesus drums the point home by saying that this man will die that same night, emphasising the ridiculousness of how the man plans to use his money.

Jesus isn't commenting on whether it's right or not to demand your fair share of a parent's inheritance, but he *is* commenting on the heart desire that might lead us to relentlessly pursue worldly wealth in this way. It might be the pursuit of an inheritance, divorce settlement, investment opportunity or property portfolio. The prosperity gospel is a false one: God does not condone, or encourage us in, the building of wealth for wealth's sake. This is not to say that it is necessarily wrong to be rich (although we know that it is harder for the rich to enter God's kingdom – Matthew 19:24), but the desire to store up more and more comfort around ourselves is not a biblical one. God is more interested in our character than our comfort, and longs for us to find contentment in him, not money. The security we feel like we're building around ourselves when we invest in earthly things is actually not very secure at all, as this parable demonstrates.

It may not be the case that your busyness is linked to a desire for more wealth or a fear of not having enough, but if it is then Jesus' teaching on money here is very relevant. The desire for more and more can make us fidgety, uneasy, anxious and fretful. When we seek to trust God for our future provision, lean into Jesus for our present contentment and ask the Holy Spirit to change our character, we will find ourselves much more able to go about the work God has given us to do with an attitude of stillness.

Prayer

- Is your busy lifestyle a result of a fear about money, either not having enough or wanting more than you currently have?

- If so, ask God to change your heart, give you contentment and provide for your future. If not, it is still good practice to ask God to provide for your needs and help you to trust him more each day.

Stillness idea

Next time you find yourself thinking about money or getting anxious about how you're going to pay the bills, stop and ask God what he wants to teach you in this moment. Perhaps keep a notebook of all the things God says to you in these moments, as there may well be a lot of them – in my experience, anxiety relating to money rarely goes away overnight! Each time you're anxious, take it to God, ask him for his perspective and jot it down in your notebook.

Reflect

After you have a few things written down, read them back and reflect: what has God been teaching you? What is the new perspective he has given you? Where is this outlined in the Bible, and can you jot down any key verses or passages? How is your attitude and character changing as you allow him to do this important work in you?

Be Still

— even when the future is unknown.

Introduction

I am very aware of how busyness can give way to worry. We have so much on our plate, so much to be concerned about, that worry layers up and up until it feels suffocating. We worry about whether we're doing enough, whether we'll have enough, whether things will end up as we want them to end up, whether we'll meet deadlines, whether we'll cope physically and mentally with the challenges facing us.

Jesus' words in our passage today offer a new perspective, a new way of looking at our lives, which leads to stillness – even when we're not sure what the future holds. Worry may come and go, anxiety may be a very real battle for us, yet God gives us what we need to be still.

Read Matthew 6:25–34

'Therefore I tell you, do not worry about your life, what you will eat or drink; or about your body, what you will wear. Is not life more than food, and the body more than clothes? Look at the birds of the air; they do not sow or reap or store away in barns, and yet your heavenly Father feeds them. Are you not much more valuable than they? Can any one of you by worrying add a single hour to your life?

'And why do you worry about clothes? See how the flowers of the field grow. They do not labour or spin. Yet I tell you that not even Solomon in all his splendour was dressed like one of these. If that is how God clothes the grass of the field, which is here today and tomorrow is thrown into the fire, will he not much more clothe you – you of little faith? So do not worry, saying, "What shall we eat?" or "What shall we drink?" or "What shall we wear?" For the pagans run after all these things, and your heavenly Father knows that you need them. But seek first his kingdom and his righteousness, and all these things will be given to you as well. Therefore do not worry about tomorrow, for tomorrow will worry about itself. Each day has enough trouble of its own.'

If we dive right into the middle of these words, we discover the world's approach to life: 'The pagans run after all these things [what to eat, drink and wear].' Society around us is chasing all sorts of goals in pursuit of joyful fulfilment. It might literally be food, drink or clothes – or it might be cars, property, holidays or gadgets. Jesus spoke these words 2,000 years ago, but nothing has changed: people still pursue the gifts of God to do for them what only God himself can do.

I think this is a helpful place to start, because it is only when considering how culture operates that we see how joyous and beautiful Jesus' offer is. It can be so easy to fall into the mindset of wanting the things we see around us. Yes, we have Jesus, but our sinful selves quickly forget what he has done and who he promises to be for us. So we slip into working hard to build an impressive property portfolio, pursuing love and marriage at any cost, or committing hours and hours to a new hobby in order to find contentment. We know only Jesus fulfils us, yet we keep checking, in case it's possible to have contentment elsewhere *as well as Jesus*.

But Jesus offers a perspective which is starkly contrasting. He tells us to not worry or chase after the things we need, because he knows and provides. Jesus' rationale is the birds of the air, who are provided with the food they need, and the flowers of the field, who look beautiful just as they are. His counsel is two-fold: we don't need to worry, because God will provide; but we also don't need to chase luxury, because God's providence is enough. The birds eat simply and the flowers are dressed simply, but this is sufficient, and our lives should be a journey of learning to rest in this sufficiency too. As long as we have food to eat and clothes to wear, Jesus is saying that is enough. His food will sustain us, even if it's not from a Michelin-starred restaurant, and his beauty will shine through us, even if our clothes aren't designer.

So what do we chase, if those around us are chasing the gifts of God? We chase his kingdom (v. 33). We run after it with all we have, desiring to learn more about who God is and seeing his righteousness grow in our lives. The amazing news? 'All these things will be given to you as well' (v. 33). I don't think this is a 'name it and claim it' scripture, but an assurance that when our eyes are on Jesus, his eyes are on us and our needs. He will provide what we require for each day – and will often provide more on top – but we receive this in Jesus' name, not because we have strived hard for it in our own strength.

It takes a lifetime of intentional Christ-focused living to live like this. I know I'm not there yet. But what a weight is lifted off when we take to heart these words, culminating in verse 34: 'Therefore do not worry about tomorrow, for tomorrow will worry about itself. Each day has enough trouble of its own.' Busy people often need to plan ahead, to ensure everything in their busy calendars gets done and gets done well. But when this slips into worry, we need to check ourselves. Today has things to worry about: are we concerning ourselves with what is presented right in front of us? Or are we missing those needs because we're too busy living in the future? We don't know what tomorrow brings – it may bring the problems we are anticipating, but chances are it will bring a whole lot of outcomes we weren't expecting too. There is no way we can accurately predict what tomorrow will look like, so Jesus is reminding us to stay focused on the here and now.

Prayer

- Is there anything you are chasing besides Jesus? Has your chasing of his kingdom been a priority for you recently?

- Bring your goals and desires to Jesus. Ask him to embed his words in this passage into your heart. Ask him to help you to chase after God's kingdom first. And declare that you trust his provision for tomorrow.

Stillness idea

Take a few minutes at the start of your day – either when you wake up or as soon as you have a moment to yourself (which might be once you get to work, once the baby is napping, once the TV is on) – and still your heart before God. Intentionally turn your thoughts towards the goodness of his kingdom and righteousness. Stay in this space for a little while, then ask God to help you keep focused on these things throughout your day.

Reflect

How did your day go as a result of starting off with your mind focused on the right things? Could this become an intentional daily habit for you?

Be Still

— even when your dreams remain unfulfilled.

Introduction

I wonder if you're a 'five-year plan' personality, with a clear idea of what you want life to look like in the future, or more of a 'seat-of-your-pants, let's see what happens' type of person. Whichever category you fall into, it's likely there is something you have in mind that you'd like to happen one day, even if it's not written into a fixed plan. Perhaps it's getting married, having children, owning your own home, starting a business or charity, reaching a particular career level or living abroad.

In the process of working towards our dreams, it's easy to envy others who are already living that dream. Attending weddings when your own dates never work out can be painful, as can holding your friend's baby when pregnancy tests never show the right result for you, or seeing a friend's travel pictures when your circumstances don't allow you to fly around the world.

If we knew for sure that our future held what we dream for in the present, it would be much easier to live with contentment. But God calls us to be still *before* we know whether those dreams will ever come into fruition.

Read Psalm 37:1–7

> Do not fret because of those who are evil
>   or be envious of those who do wrong;
> for like the grass they will soon wither,
>   like green plants they will soon die away.
> Trust in the Lord and do good;
>   dwell in the land and enjoy safe pasture.
> Take delight in the Lord,
>   and he will give you the desires of your heart.
> Commit your way to the Lord;
>   trust in him and he will do this:
> he will make your righteous reward shine like the dawn,
>   your vindication like the noonday sun.
> Be still before the Lord
>   and wait patiently for him;
> do not fret when people succeed in their ways,
>   when they carry out their wicked schemes.

Our dreams for this life can obscure what's really important in the next life. They can blur our eternal vision, obstructing from view the incredible end-point of life with God forever, which is far greater than any marriage, family life, career, travel or home-owning opportunity.

I find it incredibly moving, however, that God, who has prepared such a wonderful eternal home for us, does not harshly say, 'Stop fussing about this life; there's no comparison with the next life' – even though that's 100% true! God knows that we will be tempted by the lovely, enviable things around us, and the people who have them. 'Do not fret… or be envious' (v. 1) sounds like the gentle coaxing of a loving Father, encouraging us to remember that he has something even better lined up for us.

On the odd occasions that I take my children to a costly play centre or theme park, you can be sure that within the first few minutes I'll be inundated with requests for 'extras': candy floss from the special machine that makes it while you watch, a ride on one of those static cars that wobbles from side to side, a plastic ball filled with plastic tat from a dispenser. (What is the attraction of these?) My response is to try to help my children focus on what's actually in front of them: massive slides, ball pits, zip wires, animals, magic shows, funfair rides – not rubbish little cars or plastic tat! Having paid extortionate money to get in, I'm keen to point out to my kids all that this entrance fee entails for them. At this point my kids will invariably look up, notice their environment and run off to enjoy it. It's not that they don't want to be there; it's just that they are momentarily side-tracked by something of far lesser value and enjoyment.

I think the same can be true of us and our eternal lives. We know that heaven will be far greater than anything we could ever experience on earth, even if we can't quite comprehend what that will look like. Like my kids, it's not that we don't want to go to heaven or aren't looking forward to it, it's just that we are side-tracked by all the very many distractions here on earth. Like the overpriced candyfloss or the tiny plastic figure that doesn't fit together properly, we chase after comfort, beauty, sex, power and financial security before we look up and realise that there are much better things we could be enjoying.

The problem with the things of this world is that they are limited in how they can fulfil us, but unlimited in how much we can reach for them. You can always build more wealth, pursue more relationships, grow more ambitious. Why are entrepreneurs successful? Because they don't hit a ceiling and say, 'Right, that's enough now. I've got enough money and own enough businesses. I think I'll take it easy from now on.' No! They are constantly dreaming up new ideas and investments. It never ends – but it never satisfies.

God, on the other hand, is Alpha (beginning) and Omega (end) (Revelation 22:13). Our lives begin and end in him. Only he can totally fulfil us, to the point where we need nothing else. We just need to keep our eyes fixed on him, and our dreams submitted to his sovereignty.

Prayer

- What are the things you dream of for your future? What do you hold dear?

- God invites us to bring our desires before him (v. 4); he doesn't dismiss them. But he also invites us into a contented stillness while we're waiting (v. 7). Bring your hopes and dreams to him now, and ask him to bring his contentment to you even as they remain unfulfilled.

Stillness idea

God is our beginning and he is our end. Spend a few moments visualising this: ask God to give you a picture of 'Alpha and Omega' which works for you. Perhaps he is at the start and end of a race track or he is the bookends at either side of the stories which make up your life. You could draw the picture in a journal, if you like, as a reminder when you're feeling disappointed by unfulfilled dreams.

Reflect

How does knowing God as your 'Omega' or 'end goal' change your perspective? How is this enabling you to be still now, even when your earthly dreams and desires have not been fulfilled?

God makes us the most unbelievable offer... to be our parent. Yes, even when we're all grown up and have children of our own! But many of us don't live experiencing the connection, guidance and support that's on offer. Why? Because we've forgotten how to be a child. In this easy-to-read guide, Anna Hawken explores ten different ways to rediscover our 'child side'. She uses the living, breathing examples of the children in our lives to inspire and challenge us. Read it on your own or with others, using the individual reflections, questions and small group notes to guide you. These simple ideas will help even the busiest parent to draw closer to God.

Being God's Child: A Parent's Guide
Ten things you can learn from your kids
Anna Hawken
978 1 80039 198 7 £6.99

brfonline.org.uk

Say goodbye to exhaustion and overwhelm... In our fast-paced world, *Finding Flourishing* redefines wellbeing as an accessible daily pursuit, even for the busiest among us. Naomi Aidoo presents a practical and tangible approach to achieving wellbeing, one that doesn't require adding yet another technique to your busy schedule. Instead, it enhances your day-to-day mentally, emotionally and spiritually. Exploring wellbeing from a biblical standpoint, Aidoo considers how it might look in our relationships, our work and the rest of our lives, and uses the T.I.M.E. framework to offer manageable steps towards achieving it.

Finding Flourishing
Time and pace for your work–life wellbeing
Naomi Aidoo
978 1 80039 274 8 £8.99

brfonline.org.uk

Rhythms of Grace

Finding intimacy with God in a busy life

Tony Horsfall

Rhythms of Grace emerges from a personal exploration of contemplative spirituality. Coming from an evangelical and charismatic background, Tony Horsfall felt an increasing desire to know God more deeply. At the same time, he felt an increasing dissatisfaction with his own spiritual life, as well as concern at the number of highly qualified and gifted people involved in Christian ministry who experience burn-out. In this book he shows how contemplative spirituality, with its emphasis on realising our identity as God's beloved children and on being rather than doing, has vital lessons for us about discovering intimacy with God.

Rhythms of Grace
Finding intimacy with God in a busy life
Tony Horsfall
978 1 80039 327 1   £9.99

brfonline.org.uk

Exhaustion, burn-out, even breakdown... sadly, such conditions are all too common these days, not least among those involved in some kind of Christian ministry, whether full-time, part-time or voluntary. In striving to do our utmost for God, we can forget that there were many times when Jesus himself was willing to rest, to do nothing except wait for the Spirit's prompting, so that he demonstrated the vital principle of 'working from a place of rest'. Drawing on extensive experience of training and mentoring, Tony Horsfall reflects on the story of Jesus and the Samaritan woman to draw out practical guidance for sustainable Christian life and work.

Working from a Place of Rest
Jesus and the key to sustaining ministry
Tony Horsfall
978 1 80039 220 5 £9.99

brfonline.org.uk

Inspiring people of all ages to grow in Christian faith

BRF Ministries is the home of Anna Chaplaincy, Living Faith, Messy Church and Parenting for Faith

As a charity, our work would not be possible without fundraising and gifts in wills.
To find out more and to donate,
visit brf.org.uk/give or call +44 (0)1235 462305